Pursuit Excellence Through Cont. Process Improvement

- Best Practices
  need to move from
  Know How to Know why
  so we can cope with the application to your
  case & future cases.

A True engineer   P 103

Good Mgr vs Engr
- Spellbound by Technical Perfection vs   P108
  Business Judgement That it is
  The level of improvement I need

- How Things 'Ought' to be Done to Trying it.
p55 I know we have Golfers in the Audience I checked
The signups, you all know the Golfer that looks Good
& Talks a big Game. - but ultimately you have to hit
the Ball.
    Its not about form or how thing ought to be
it About Doing it & learning & Doing it again and learning

THE SAYINGS OF SHIGEO SHINGO

Key Strategies for Plant Improvement

Shigeo Shingo

THE SAYINGS OF SHIGEO SHINGO
Key Strategies for Plant Improvement

SHIGEO SHINGO

Translated by
Andrew P. Dillon

With a foreword by
Norman Bodek
President, Productivity, Inc.

Originally published by Nikkan Kōgyō Shimbun, Ltd.

Productivity Press
Portland, Oregon

Originally published as *Shingo goroku: kōjō kaizen no hiketsu o kataru*, copyright
©1985 by the Nikkan Kogyo Shimbun, Ltd., Tokyo.

English translation copyright © 1987 by Productivity Press, a division of
Productivity, Inc.

Productivity Press
P.O. Box 13390
Portland, OR   97213-0390
Telephone: (503) 235-0600
Telefax: (503) 235-0909
E-mail: service@ppress.com

Printed and bound by BookCrafters
Printed in the United States of America

Library of Congress Cataloging-in-Publication Data

Shingō, Shigeo, 1909–1990
     The sayings of Shigeo Shingō
     Translation of: Shingō goroku/Shingō Shigeo.
     Includes index.
     ISBN 0-915299-15-1
     1. Production management. I. Title.
TS155.S46213   1987
658.5   87-60547
                                                                            CIP

02 01 00 99 98   12 11 10 9 8 7

Foreword

If I could give a Nobel prize for exceptional contributions to world economy, prosperity, and productivity, I wouldn't have much difficulty selecting a winner — Shigeo Shingo's life work has contributed to the well-being of everyone in the world. Along with Taiichi Ohno, former vice president of Toyota Motors, Mr. Shingo has helped revolutionize the way we manufacture goods. His improvement principles vastly reduce the cost of manufacturing — which means more products to more people; they make the manufacturing process more responsive while opening the way to new and innovative products, substantially reduce defects and improve quality, and give us a strategy for continuous improvement through the creative involvement of all employees.

In this book, Mr. Shingo shares the creative process that helped him build this significant contribution to manufacturing excellence. Inside the factory, Mr. Shingo's never-ending spirit of inquiry challenges the status quo at every level — he knows that everything can be improved. When he hears the phrases "can't be done," "we always did it that way," or "impossible," Shingo chuckles and stops and then helps the worker, manager, or corporate executive find a proper solution. In *The Sayings of Shigeo Shingo* the reader will find numerous examples of how Shingo confronted and overcame problems that seemed virtually impossible to solve.

In May 1986 Mr. Shingo gave a seminar at Ford Motor Company's Van Dyke plant, where he was shown a punch press that took five hours to change over. After a lecture of several hours and a challenge from Mr. Shingo, the die was changed in twelve minutes. Mr. Shingo was not satisfied with Van Dyke's accomplishment, however — he wanted it done in less than ten minutes. Subsequently, in

February 1987, plant manager Gifford Brown wrote us that the time had been reduced to two and a half minutes! Isn't it amazing what proper understanding can do?

Reducing changeovers from hours to minutes is an essential first step toward revolutionary change in the work place. We have seen it result in 90 percent inventory reduction, lead-time reduction from twelve weeks to four hours, quality defects down 97 percent, and so on. Shortening setup times, however, is only a small part of Mr. Shingo's achievements.

Study of Toyota Production System from an Industrial Engineering Standpoint was the first book in English to introduce us to just-in-time production and kanban techniques; *A Revolution in Manufacturing: The SMED System* gave us detailed instruction on reducing changeover times from hours to minutes; and *Zero Quality Control: Source Inspection and the Poka-yoke System* showed us how to eliminate defects totally from the manufacturing process. Now *The Sayings of Shigeo Shingo* presents through case studies the principles of continuous improvement in the workplace, a unified approach Mr. Shingo calls his *scientific thinking mechanism for improvement*.

Each October, Mr. Shingo sits down and plans for the following twelve months. Every work day is filled with a seminar or a plant visit; his consulting travels have taken him throughout Japan and to the United States, Canada, Brazil, France, and many other nations. In a typical day, Mr. Shingo travels to a client's plant, gives a short lecture, reviews some problems, and offers recommendations for solutions. That evening in his hotel room, he writes down in detail the events of the day. Over the years his disciplined, methodical approach and careful notes have provided the basis for 18 books and numerous articles on factory improvement.

On a recent Productivity study mission to Japan, we visited Matsushita's washing machine and vacuum cleaner plants. At each we were shown improvements resulting from Mr. Shingo's advice. Both plants claim that not a single defect leaves their premises. Osaka Diamond, Toyota Gosei, Arakawa Shaktai, Tsuta Kikai, Kinzoku Kogyo, and Saga Tekko are just a few of the many companies where managers credit Mr. Shingo as the teacher and catalyst to their improvement activities: "Mr. Shingo taught us how to do that!"

What makes this book so powerful is Mr. Shingo's ability to transmit knowledge to the reader step by step, through concrete examples. Mr. Shingo's approach to problems and solutions is usually quite simple and always brilliant. In example after example, he exposes the typically narrow and limited way we look at problems; and time after time he proves that there is *never* just one right answer. Mr. Shingo teaches us that there are many paths to the top of Mt. Fuji — many ways to find and make improvement.

Right now, many American companies are closing their plants and outsourcing manufacturing to the Far East in search of cheaper labor; meanwhile foreign companies buy those same closed U.S. plants to manufacture here and take advantage of our "cheap" labor. In Indiana alone, 25 plants will be opened by the Japanese in 1987. This is amazing when you realize that labor is often only 15 percent or less of manufacturing cost. Since just-in-time production can easily offset those labor costs, it is ironic that American companies are giving up the tremendous opportunities that await them in their own back yards.

Many of those opportunities are represented in the philosophy and practical techniques illustrated in this book. You will discover for yourself how to change the environment in your plant, improve the quality of your products, reduce manufacturing costs, and, most importantly, develop a consciousness that promotes daily, continuous improvement.

I want to thank Mr. Shingo for his continual quest for manufacturing excellence. I'd also like to thank Nikkan Kogyo Shimbun for permission to publish this book in English and especially Mr. Ryomatsu Sakata for his invaluable help. Andrew P. Dillon, who has translated all of Mr. Shingo's other works available in English from Productivity, has provided us with another excellent, accurate translation. Thanks also to Connie Dyer and Nancy MacMillan, who edited the manuscript, and to Patty Slote, production manager, Marie Kascus, indexer, and finally to Nanette Redmond, Caroline Kutil, James Rolwing, Laura Santi, and Leslie Goldstein of Rudra Press, who typeset the text, prepared the artwork, and designed the book.

Norman Bodek

Contents

Introduction

SETTING OUT ON THE ROAD TO PLANT IMPROVEMENT

Scientific management was introduced in Japan in 1907 with the publication of a complete translation by Hoshino Yukinori of Frederick W. Taylor's classic work, *The Principles of Scientific Management*. Later, in the second decade of this century, a series of his shorter pieces, translated by Ikeda Fujishirō (under the title *Eliminating Unprofitable Effort*), gained enormous popularity and is said to have contributed significantly to the dissemination of scientific principles.

My own initial encounter with plant improvement work took place in 1925 when in high school I read and was deeply impressed by Fujishirō's book *Tips for Eliminating Unprofitable Effort*.

In 1930, after graduating from Yamanashi Technical College, I went to work at the Taipei Railway Factory belonging to the Government-General of Taiwan. Japanese railway plants had been first in Japan to introduce scientific principles in a systematic fashion; they could repair railway cars in a mere five days, disassembling locomotives and replacing all steam pipes or remachining all cylinders. The same procedure took three times as long at the Taiwan Railway plant, and I wondered what accounted for the difference. I thought at the time it might have something to do with labor costs.

Comparing actual values, however, I found a gap of only about 20 percent. I suspected that this alone could not account for the difference in repair times. After looking into the matter, I noticed that our management methods differed, and I began to study the books on plant management and related topics.

In 1931, I ran across a translation of Taylor's book in a neighborhood bookstore. Thumbing through it, I found a most unusual statement. "Inexpensive goods," it said, "can be produced even when workers are paid high wages." The apparent impossibility of such a proposition aroused my suspicions, and as I continued to leaf through the book, I saw that Taylor claimed the feat was possible if efficiency was raised to a high level.

For me, this argument was utterly novel, so I bought the book and did not sleep until I had read it from cover to cover. At that point I resolved to devote my life to scientific management.

Since then, I have studied many works on the subject, including Professor Ueno Yōichi's books on efficiency, the journals of the Japan Industry Association and the Japan Efficiency League — *Industry and Economics* and *Industrial Efficiency*, respectively — and documents from the Provisional Bureau for Rationalizing Industry. At the time of my resolve, I issued an appeal to young technicians at the railway plant and organized "scientific management study sessions." Five years later, as a result of our plant improvement efforts, we had shortened repair times to ten days, increased productivity considerably, and implemented numerous operational improvements.

By chance, I learned that the first full-term Production Technology Seminar sponsored by the Japan Industry Association was to be held in Tokyo and applied to attend at my own expense. As one of five participants, I commuted to the training site at Unozawa Iron Works plant from an apartment near Tokyo's Ebisu railway station where I lived with the wife I had married in April of that same year.

From Professor Horikome Ken'ichi, we learned such techniques as motion analysis, work analysis, and process analysis. During the first month, however, we concentrated on motion analysis, emphasizing mastery of concepts rather than techniques. Frank B. Gilbreth's "motion mind" philosophy was thoroughly drilled into us, i.e., the notion that one can discover the single best method by breaking work down into elements that are then thoroughly analyzed. Day in and day out, we prepared motion analyses and came up with ideas for improvement. Our ideas were then criticized by Professor Horikome.

This experience forms the backbone of my philosophy; it is the foundation for my lifelong commitment to pursue improvement to its source. My thinking is based on Frederick Taylor's analytical philosophy and under Professor Horikome's tutelage it has been deeply colored by Frank Gilbreth's exhaustive pursuit of goals and the single best method. Indeed, this has been the basic thrust of my own (IE) industrial engineering improvement courses.

I returned to Taiwan after attending the course and put all my efforts into carrying out improvements. As a result, we achieved success nearly unparalleled in the entire Japanese railway system. In 1943, I was transferred to a production plant for aerial torpedo depth gauges and succeeded in doubling production within six months. I also began working for the Japan Management Association in 1945, concentrating on IE education and plant improvement surveys. That same year, during an improvement survey at the Kasato plant of Hitachi, Ltd., I clarified the nature of production by defining it for the first time as a *network of processes and operations*.

Later, in 1956, at the Mitsubishi Heavy Industries' Nagasaki shipyards, we set a world's record by shortening hull construction time for the *World Independence* from four to three months and then to two months. The methods we used helped carry Japan to the forefront of the shipbuilding industry worldwide.

After concluding a three-year improvement survey at Mitsubishi Heavy Industries between 1956 and 1958, I left the Japan Management Association to found the Institute for Management Improvement. My aim was to improve basic conceptual approaches and methods rather than merely to improve techniques. This philosophy led me in 1967 to develop source inspection and the poka-yoke system and the zero quality control system for the total elimination of defects. In 1969, during an improvement survey at Toyota Motors, I developed SMED (single-minute exchange of die — or machine setups in under 10 minutes) which cut setup time on a 1,000-ton press, for example, from four hours to three minutes.

Since then, I have studied many works on improvement. In particular, I learned various methods of idea development from Professor Ueda Yōichi's *Methods for Developing Creativity* (in Japanese). I learned to distinguish between ideas and judgments from A. F. Osborn's *Brainstorming*, and I learned approaches to use when implementing improvement ideas from Dale Carnegie's *How to Win Friends and Influence People*. These books have all influenced the way I conduct improvement surveys. I kept thinking, over the years, however, that these general concepts and specific techniques did not necessarily add up to a comprehensive approach to improvement.

To extend and enhance this approach, I developed STM — a *scientific thinking mechanism for the purpose of improvement*. STM is a unified, systematic mechanism of mental processes and methods that involves locking in on a problem, brainstorming, judgment, proposal, and finally, implementation. I believe that anyone can use this mechanism to carry out improvements better, faster, and more easily.

Having conceived the idea around 1970, I wrote a book on the subject in 1980, *Systematic Thinking for Plant Improvement* (in Japanese).

This volume is a series of pieces from a three-year period that appeared in the monthly journal *Plant Management* (in Japanese), in response to requests from many people who attended my basic IE course. I have also included a number of examples postdating the publication of *Systematic Thinking for Plant Improvement*. Rather than merely presenting a succession of case studies, I arranged examples to correspond to each stage of the scientific thinking mechanism for improvement. This means that in some places I have cited material from my earlier books, so I beg the indulgence of my readers. [Editor's Note: A list of Mr. Shingo's publications, in Japanese and English, follows the *Afterword*].

Nothing will make me happier if this book is of some relevance or provides suggestions to those whose goal is plant improvement.

Shigeo Shingo

THE SAYINGS OF
SHIGEO SHINGO

Key Strategies for
Plant Improvement

1
A Scientific Thinking Mechanism for Improvement

Many improvement philosophies and techniques advocated in the past address only parts or aspects of a problem and have failed to be comprehensive and systematic. I propose a scientific approach to thinking through problems (STM) that combines these various philosophies and techniques in a systematic way. A schematic outline of this STM is given in Figure 1 and the suggestions I make throughout the book follow the categories shown.

THE RELATIONSHIP BETWEEN STM AND TECHNIQUES FOR RATIONALIZING PRODUCTION

Various techniques have been proposed to make production more rational. These methods are classified below on the basis of their characteristics.

Analytic and Quantitative Methods for Assessing the Status Quo

The following methods allow us to get a grip on the status quo — to *improve* the conditions we find, we need to think about them scientifically and systematically using STM.

1. *Motion analysis*: analysis of motions themselves
2. *Time analysis*: temporal analysis
3. *Work analysis*: analysis of work done by humans or machines
4. *Process analysis*: analysis of the course of changes undergone by products
5. *Work factor (WF), methods time management (MTM) analysis*:

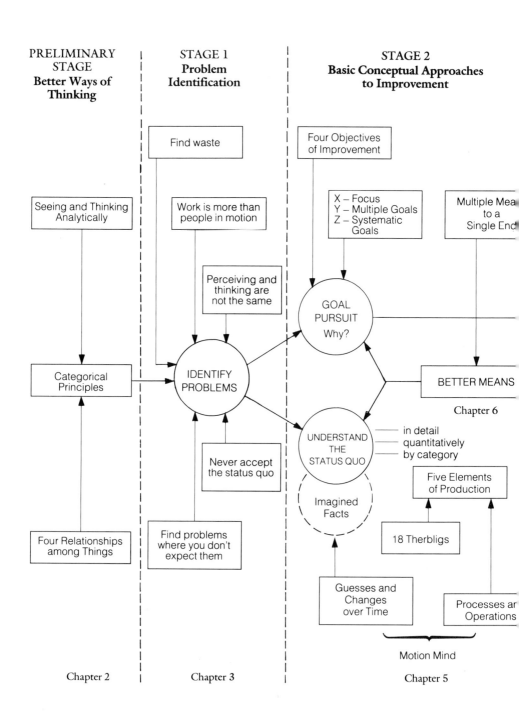

FIGURE 1. Scientific Thinking Mechanism

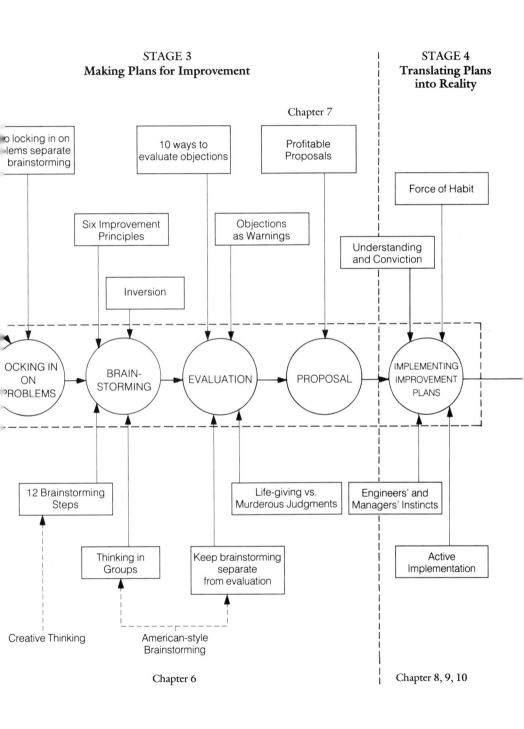

STAGE 3
Making Plans for Improvement

STAGE 4
**Translating Plans
into Reality**

Chapter 7

o locking in on
lems separate
brainstorming

10 ways to
evaluate objections

Profitable
Proposals

Force of Habit

Six Improvement
Principles

Objections
as Warnings

Understanding
and Conviction

Inversion

OCKING IN
ON
ROBLEMS

BRAIN-
STORMING

EVALUATION

PROPOSAL

IMPLEMENTING
IMPROVEMENT
PLANS

12 Brainstorming
Steps

Life-giving vs.
Murderous Judgments

Engineers' and
Managers' Instincts

Thinking in
Groups

Keep brainstorming
separate
from evaluation

Active
Implementation

Creative Thinking

American-style
Brainstorming

Chapter 6

Chapter 8, 9, 10

operation time analysis with the addition of leveling (evaluation of human work averages)

6. *Work sampling*: an analytical method that borrows sampling techniques from statistics to make measurement easier

7. *Control charts*: a method that makes it easy to grasp the current state of quality

8. *Histograms*: a method of grasping the current state of quality quantitatively

Methods That Provide Clear Objectives and Motivate People

Rather than merely telling people to work better, it is much more productive to set out clear objectives and to provide motivation.

Management by objectives (MBO). No matter how effective it may be to set clear objectives and then strive to achieve them, bursts of effort alone won't do the trick; in the final analysis, methods must be improved.

Zero defects (ZD). A ZD campaign aimed at cutting defects to zero is a kind of management by objectives. To attain those objectives, however, requires an approach to improvement that goes beyond simple awareness of the problem and conventional modes of thinking.

Work design. In industrial engineering, improvements are based on the status quo. Work-design techniques, on the other hand, advocate seeking absolute measures — starting from zero in terms of materials, labor, and all other cost, and permitting only the minimum required costs. This enables us to pursue higher-level goals than are possible with improvement methods that start with the current situation as a base. In this respect, work-design techniques are undoubtedly effective tools. To identify the absolute minimum means needed, however, requires a thinking mechanism that is rigorous and systematic.

Methods for Setting Standards Rationally

It is natural to want to set standards rationally. It seems to me, however, that theoretical pursuits tend to become goals in themselves, and people forget that those pursuits are merely a means for rationalizing production. In other words, management can end up subordinated to the pursuit of mathematical methods.

Statistical quality control (SQC or SPC). Looking over published works on quality control (QC), I cannot help thinking that too many pages are devoted to mathematical and statistical processing methods for setting standards. Isn't this the prime reason most supervisors on the shop floor consider QC difficult to understand? Quality control should never be confined to scholarly theoretical studies; it has to be comprehensible to ordinary managers and shop-floor supervisors.

No doubt it is a valid perception that much of Japan's success in achieving high levels of quality is the result of workers' improvement activities, such as QC circles. Now, however, we must recognize the importance of total quality control (TQC) involving every individual and division within the enterprise.

We are also discovering that most defects occur not because of improperly set standards, but as the result of errors in control and execution. Surely, the fact that source inspection and the poka-yoke system permit continuous zero-defect production in so many plants bears eloquent testimony to this assertion. There is still considerable room, however, for further improvement by applying STM.

Quality management (QM). QM has achieved considerable popularity recently. Like SQC, it elevates the importance of setting standards — in itself a perfectly justifiable position. Yet if we want to make the production shop more efficient, the question of which sort of evaluation is appropriate is a bit beside the point. This method is undoubtedly useful for firms, such as those in the chemical industry, which are significantly influenced by whether standards are set correctly. I think it is important, however, to stay alert to the danger of allowing scholarly interests to dictate methods that are of little use in actually improving shop efficiency.

Value engineering (VE) and value analysis (VA). Lawrence D. Miles's concepts of value engineering and value analysis define value as function in relation to cost and call for the thorough study of both function and cost issues. The scientific thinking mechanism for improvement — as an approach that analyzes the status quo, pursues ends, and recognizes multiple means to a single end — can also be effectively applied to the goal of achieving value.

It is also necessary, however, to use a scientific approach in applying categorical principles and modes of problem awareness — especially locking in on problems, brainstorming, judging, and making proposals — and in implementing suggested improvements in the workplace.

The economic lot. The economic lot theory makes the rational claim that the burden of setup times is reduced as processing-lot size increases but that, since on the other hand this causes stocks to increase, a balance must be struck between the two factors. This calculation, however, has been rendered effectively worthless by the concept of SMED (single-minute exchange of die), which can reduce setup times from four hours to three minutes. Implementing SMED effectively also involves the application of a scientific thinking mechanism.

Materials requirements planning (MRP). Many plants are adopting some form of MRP to set optimum order points and order amounts for parts and materials. Computers are being used to make these determinations. On the other hand, SMED makes extremely small installment deliveries possible; and one-piece flows can reduce lead time from days down to hours.

What effect, then, does MRP have when production methods themselves can be improved? The scientific thinking mechanism for improvement can be used to implement SMED and dramatically shorten lead times.

Rationalization of Means

The term *rationalization* sometimes refers simply to making means rational rather than to making goals or ends rational. For example, human work becomes easier and productivity surges when manual functions are augmented by tools, and again when these tools are mechanized and automated. Human labor has been made even easier and production further increased by developments that include:

- machining centers that replace tools automatically
- numerical control (NC) machines that automate dimension settings and carry out compound operations automatically
- robots that automate manual operations

In many of these cases, however, only *means* have been rationalized while rationalization of *ends* — the thorough improvement of operating methods — has been neglected. This point requires extensive reconsideration but, in either event, improvement is more effectively pursued by invoking the scientific thinking mechanism.

Computers. This is the age of almighty computers, performing complex calculations at overwhelming speeds with immense memories.

At a certain American firm, I heard the boast that even with extensive stocks, a three-dimensional automatic warehouse made it possible to retrieve a needed part within three minutes. When my hosts inserted a card in a computer, the indicated part did in fact arrive within three minutes. Yet when I compared this company with one at which adoption of a stockless production system had eliminated the need for warehouses, I wondered which company had more truly rationalized its operations.

Preventive maintenance (PM). When we follow the principles of preventive maintenance, machines are maintained so thoroughly that no breakdowns occur. Using the scientific thinking mechanism in applying these principles can be extremely effective. At the same time, we must not forget to consider the rationalization of ends — to ask *how* machines should be used to rationalize production.

* * * * * * *

These are some of the techniques used to rationalize production that can be enhanced through the application of the scientific thinking mechanism for improvement (STM). I want to stress the continuing fundamental need, in aiming for rationalization, for a systematic, scientific approach to improvement. The chapters that follow contain specific suggestions that illustrate different aspects of that improvement process.

2
Preliminary Stage: Basic Ways of Thinking

CATEGORICAL PRINCIPLES

Categorical principles guide our thinking and help us classify ideas and observations.

There Are Many Categorical Principles in the World

There are many categorical principles, and consequently many different classifications are possible. For example, humans may be classified in a number of ways:

men versus *women*: sex
those who wear glasses versus *those who don't*: visual acuity
adults versus *children*: age
sick people versus *healthy people*: health

Phenomena Can Be Classified Either Continuously or by Opposition

For example, in the classification *men* and *women*, all people who are not men are women, and all people who are not women are men. This classification is extremely clear and simple because a division into only two categories is involved: *A* or *not A*. *In the case of adults* and *children*, however, the categorical principle of "age" is continuous: it could be 1, 2, 3 ... 10, 20, 30, etc. It becomes difficult to draw the line between adult and child, and the division must be established by convention. Here, a *numerical limit* must be clearly defined.

It is important to understand this distinction because in our own cases involving continuous phenomena such as color gradations or the severity of flaws, classification is extremely difficult unless standards for deciding are shown by means of numerical values and limit samples. Even with a limit sample, it can be quite difficult to determine whether a phenomenon immediately adjacent to the limit is acceptable or not.

Avoid Intersecting Divisions

Intersecting division means applying two categorical principles in a single classification. For example, suppose I have the following files:

- items for automobiles
- items for trucks
- steel items
- nonsteel items

I would not know where to file "steel materials for automobiles," because I am trying to apply the two categorical principles, body type and material type, at the same time. In a case like this, I must apply categorical principles consecutively, one after another. Thus, I might have:

- *first-order categorical principle*: body type
- *second-order categorical principle*: material type

Here, within the automobile file there would be a further division into steel items and nonsteel items.

Thus, not only is the categorical principle a basic and extremely important notion for classification, but the principles themselves must always be rigorously clarified when implementing ideas for improvement.

To sum up, then:

- Adopt multiple ways of viewing categorical principles.
- Consider the nature of the phenomena in question, i.e., whether they can be classified by opposition or continuously.
- Always avoid intersecting divisions. Problems will resist resolution unless consecutive categorical principles are applied.

Broken Down

FOUR RELATIONSHIPS AMONG THINGS

There Are Only Four Relationships Among Things

The world contains billions of people and things, and as a result, relationships among those people and things must be nearly infinite. First, however, these relationships can be divided into two categories: related and unrelated.

Where objects are related, the relationships are restricted to four kinds:

1. *Cause-and-Effect*: "The fire was started by a cigarette butt."
2. *Opposition*: "fire and water"
3. *Similarity*: "wooden shelf and steel shelf"
4. *Proximity*: "table and chair"

I use the following examples to help me remember these relationships:

1. *Cause-and-Effect*: parent and child
2. *Opposition*: husband and wife, in the sense of man and woman.
3. *Similarity*: sibling and sibling
4. *Proximity*: friend and friend

Keeping these relations in mind helps us analyze a variety of phenomena. We may consider a number of important questions:

- Is anything causing the phenomenon under consideration?
- Does anything oppose it?
- Is anything similar to it?
- Does anything always appear in conjunction with it?

This line of thinking can be of particular help when we develop cause diagrams for quality control.

Objects Are Either Concrete or Abstract

An *object* may be either concrete or abstract. A concrete object can be apprehended by means of one or more of the five senses: sight, touch, hearing, smell, and taste. Abstract objects, in contrast, are *relationships* — between concrete objects, between concrete and abstract objects, or between abstract objects.

A technical worker is said to work on *concrete* objects, whereas someone in finance, for example, is said to work on *abstract* objects. Even when products are actually being made, however, the technical worker's function of standing by the machine is also abstract. Thus, while concrete objects are comprehensible enough, it is often difficult to perceive abstract objects.

Consequently, when it comes to carrying out improvement, effective results cannot be achieved by dealing only with visible, tangible objects; we must also exhaustively pursue our true objectives — the abstract objects lying beyond what is visible.

ANALYTICAL WAYS OF SEEING AND THINKING

We get closer to the truth by analyzing and observing objects in detail. It is important always to observe and think analytically when pursuing facts or goals.

Forgetting — And Forgetting You Have Forgotten

Since human beings are not omniscient, we occasionally forget things. We can at least try not to forget that we have forgotten, however. If we manage this, it will ultimately be as though we had not forgotten.

This is why we use checklists. Checklists would be unnecessary if people never forgot things. Production workers who forget to attach parts or mistakenly attach the wrong parts are scolded by their supervisors and urged to pay more attention. Yet, this is as good as asking workers to become God. Can we say we have never forgotten anything in our lives? *Poka-yoke* (mistake-proofing) recognizes that since as humans we will inevitably forget things, we should at least make certain we don't forget that we have forgotten. This not only makes things easier; it is a shortcut that makes attainment of zero defects a certainty.

Knowledge, Understanding, and Ability Are Different

We think we "know" certain things we perceive. This does not mean, however, that we have really "understood" them. Understanding demands more than simply knowing. It means we have examined what we know from all angles and found out why it has to be the way it is. Understanding results from a multifaceted examination and includes the realization that the phenomenon in question must be the way it is.

This by itself is not enough, however; we must also have *ability*. All our knowledge and understanding won't get us anywhere unless we are able to act on it. Our plans for improvement may be magnificent, but whether they show actual results will depend ultimately on ability.

3

Stage One: Problem Identification

Problem identification, the first step in making improvements, involves the following concepts:

- Never accept the status quo.
- Find problems where you think none exist.
- Work is more than people in motion.
- Perceiving and thinking are not the same.

NEVER ACCEPT THE STATUS QUO

People who are satisfied with the way things are can never achieve improvement or progress. Indeed, the first step in improvement is dissatisfaction with the status quo; it means always asking why productivity can't be increased, why stocks are necessary, or whether there aren't better ways to do things.

We often voice our complaints and dissatisfaction. According to Mr. Harada, managing director of the Sailor Pen Company, however, dissatisfaction rankles more than complaints. A human being with no dissatisfaction will never make any progress. Problem awareness will never occur in the person who is utterly without discontent, who says he is satisfied.

Even among those who feel dissatisfaction, however, there are some who blame it on the fact that they must contend with high-diversity, low-volume production, or that they must produce in response to orders, or that plant equipment is outdated. In these people, who ascribe problems mainly to external factors and make no move to resolve them through their own efforts, dissatisfaction has changed to complaining. By the same token, people are on the road to progress when, on their own initiative, they try to face such problems head on.

17

It is a universal truth that those who are not dissatisfied will never make any progress. Yet even if one feels dissatisfaction, it must not be diverted into complaining; it must be actively linked to improvement. In this sense, we can say that *dissatisfaction is the mother of improvement.*

FIND PROBLEMS WHERE YOU THINK NONE EXIST

When I walk through a production workshop, workers never call out to tell me about waste or to raise questions about inefficient operations. If I just kept my mouth shut and walked through the shop, we would conclude that there were no problems at all. Obviously, this would be no good. Rather than zipping through the shop like a sightseer, looking only at the surface of things, it is better to spend an hour or even half an hour observing a machine that is thought to have no problems. If you have the attitude that there probably are some problems, you will inevitably find some. To accept the likelihood of problems is a challenge, but adopting this perspective will allow you to outpace ordinary companies.

Find Waste

Eliminate waste! This slogan is often shouted by management, yet we won't find much of what we imagine as waste lying around in the workplace. Unfortunately, real waste lurks in forms that do not look like waste. Only through careful observation and goal orientation can waste be identified. We must always keep in mind that *the greatest waste is waste we don't see.*

Pay Money for Banana Skins?

I once went to a fruit seller and paid ¥500 for a bunch of bananas. When I got home, it occurred to me that although I could eat the fruit, I certainly could not eat the skins. Yet the fruit seller had asked to be paid on the basis of bananas he weighed with the skins on. My bunch of bananas with skins weighed 2.6 kg, but the fruit without the skins weighed 1.6 kg — exactly 60 percent of the total. Why, I wondered, should I pay 100 percent of the price when only 60 percent is edible?

In the same way, we can distinguish between two types of work:

- *Work that increases value* = fruit
- *Work that only increases cost* = skin

We can think of these as follows:

- *Work that increases value:* processing, i.e., actually machining products
- *Work that only increases cost:* transport, delay, and inspection, attaching and removing products.

Just as no one really resents paying for the banana skins, we do not question what goes on in the workplace. Even when most of the work only increases cost and little is done to increase value, we become habituated to the situation, satisfied that a good job is being done if the work is performed conscientiously. Frequently we do not perceive the *intrinsic value* of the work. We must take another hard look at work and recognize what is fruit and what is skin.

"Eliminate Waste!" Is a Nonsensical Slogan

The slogan "Eliminate Waste" is posted in many plants I have visited. Once, when I saw this sign, I asked the firm's president if all his employees were idiots.

"Why do you say that?" he responded. I pointed to the slogan posted on the wall.

"But isn't it good to get rid of waste?" he asked. I asked him whether the sign was on the wall because some workers would not get rid of waste even if they saw it.

"It seems to me," I said, "that as long as someone *knows* that something constitutes waste, he will get rid of it. The big problem is not noticing that something really *is* wasteful." The slogan posted, I told him, ought to be "*Find* Waste!"

WORK IS MORE THAN PEOPLE IN MOTION

In the Japanese writing system, the character for *work* is composed of two elements, meaning, respectively, *person* and *move*. Indeed, there is a tendency to think that when people are in motion they are working. This is hardly true, however. At another level of analysis, the same written character is composed of three elements:

person + *weight* + *strength*

This is the real meaning of work: "a person exerts strength on a weighty task."

Thus, rather than assuming that a man in motion is working, we must be sure to ask whether he is really exerting his strength on some task that will produce added value.

All substances on earth are composed of a mere 104 elements, e.g. oxygen, nitrogen, and hydrogen; or gold, silver, and copper, etc.

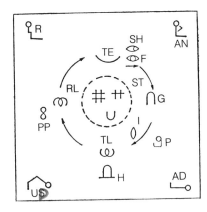

FIGURE 2. The 18 "Therbligs"

Frank B. Gilbreth studied human motion and discovered basic elements of motion, which he called *therbligs*. All human movements, he discovered, are composed of a mere 18 therbligs. These 18 elements of motion are organized as illustrated in Figure 2.

1. In the center are:
   A — *Assemble*
   DA — *Disassemble*
   U — *Use*

2. Around these are:
   TE — *Transport empty*
   G — *Grasp*
   TL — *Transport loaded*
   RL — *Release load*

3. Subsidiary to these are:
   SH — *Search*
   F — *Find*
   ST — *Select*
   P — *Reposition*
   H — *Hold*
   I — *Inspect*
   PP — *Pre-position*

4. Outside these are:
   R — *Rest*
   PN — *Plan*
   UD — *Unavoidable delay*
   AD — *Avoidable delay*

From birth to death, the argument goes, humans simply repeat these 18 elements of motion. Obviously, there are infinite variations, depending on what is being held and on the number and combinations of motion. Nevertheless, at the abstract level of motion, there are no more than 18 such elements.

Ranks in the old Japanese army were organized as follows:

Commander grade
• general
• lieutenant-general
• major-general

Field grade
- colonel
- lieutenant-colonel
- major

Subordinate grade
- captain
- first lieutenant
- second lieutenant

My rank was that of a tank corps second lieutenant. Using a similar approach to evaluating grades of motion elements, we might obtain the following scheme:

1. *Assemble, disassemble,* and *use* are basically elements of motion that increase value — the generals — and can be labeled commander grade.

2. *Transport empty, grasp, transport loaded,* and *release load* are merely elements for transporting objects and, rather than increasing value, they generally increase only cost. Still, in many cases, work cannot be accomplished without these elements of motion, and although they are of low value, they are the most frequently occurring therbligs — the true field grade elements of motion.

3. *Search, find,* and *select* occur because objects are poorly arranged or mixed together. *Reposition* is due to faulty placement.

   Hold, moreover, is a therblig resulting from poor timing. *Inspect* is an element that occurs in order to ascertain whether *assemble, disassemble,* and *use* have been performed correctly.

   In addition, *pre-position* is an element of motion for positioning an object correctly for the next cycle.

   The value of all these elements of motion — corresponding to the subordinate grade — is a grade lower than that of the other therbligs. Such elements should be kept to a minimum.

4. A task should not be so fatiguing that it requires *rest,* nor should it demand that you *plan* frequently. Nor should *unavoidable delays* be frequent, nor obviously, should workers slack off due to *avoidable delays*. Therbligs of this sort have no

"officer rank" at all, so we may refer to them as second class privates.

Since there are four grades of motion, striving to eliminate everything except value-adding motion, *assemble, disassemble*, and *use*, is ultimately linked to the assertion that *work* means "people exerting strength to accomplish weighty tasks."

PERCEIVING AND THINKING ARE NOT THE SAME

Perceiving means recognizing phenomena by means of our five senses. *Thinking*, on the other hand, is our mental ability to pursue causes and purposes by objectively asking "why" about all phenomena.

Humans *perceive* via the five senses — sight, hearing, touch, smell, and taste. Looking up at the sky, we perceive that it is cloudy. Then there is *thought*: Will it rain or not?

Here is a little story that illustrates this point:

Foreman A walks into plant manager Ohara's office with a safety part and says that a defect has occurred. "What do we do?" he asks.

Ohara examines the part for a moment and then instructs the foreman to bring him the next defective item if the defect shows up again. Dubious because he has received no instructions on how to handle the matter, the foreman goes back to the shop floor.

A week later, the defect shows up again and the foreman immediately rushes to the plant manager's office. "We've got another defect" he announces. But when the manager asks him about the conditions under which the defect occurred, the foreman stammers incoherently.

"In that case," the manager says, "bring the offending part to me if the defect shows up again." The foreman quickly withdraws.

Ten days later, when the defect occurs again, the foreman visits the manager's office for a third time. "The defect was caused by play in a stopper on the machine," he reports. "We've fixed it so the defect won't show up again."

Here's what happened: The first two times, the foreman merely *perceived* that a defect had occurred. The third time, having understood what the manager had in mind, he *thought* about why the defect might have occurred.

Thus there are two positions we can take: merely perceiving —

or thinking objectively about what we have perceived. Action comes about in response to cycling back and forth between perceiving and thinking, perceiving and thinking, and then finally, perceiving the solution. The more this cycle of perceiving and thinking is repeated, the closer we can approach the truth.

We must remember to ask ourselves, as we move from thought to action in the course of every day, whether we are merely perceiving or whether we have really thought about the matter in question.

The IBM Slogan

Some years ago, when I visited IBM as a participant in a study mission, I was impressed to see the slogan THINK posted everywhere in the plant. I asked a question of our guide after the tour. I had heard of IBM's famous slogan some time ago, I said, and I was truly impressed to see how prominently displayed it was throughout the plant. "But what on earth," I asked, "is THINK supposed to mean?"

I was given the following answer. Whenever a problem crops up at IBM, a worker doesn't go right in to the department head's office and report the problem without first thinking about it himself. The worker goes over the problem at least three times by himself and only then does he consult the department head.

The instant I heard this explanation, it struck me that at IBM, when you catch a fish, you do not take it right away to the department head and ask him how it should be cooked. You must first clean it, scale it, and wash it, and then ask how it will be cooked. Even today, the THINK slogan has left a deep impression on me. When a problem shows up, you should try to reach a solution by *thinking* about it yourself, at least three times, rather than immediately consulting your superior — as so many people do — after simply having *perceived* that a problem has occurred. This is the proper attitude — that you consult your superior only when the problem still seems insoluble.

The Brain Has Thirty-two Folds

Scholars tell us that inside the human head are two types of brain, the temporal lobe and the frontal lobe. Figure 3 shows cross sections of the heads of a gorilla, Java man, and modern man. Cerebral physiologists say that a comparison of the three shows that there are no great differences in the temporal lobes, but that the frontal lobe of Java man is larger than the gorilla's, and that of modern man is markedly larger still.

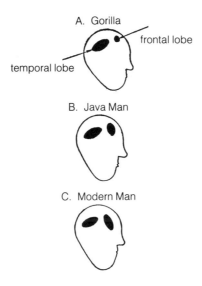

FIGURE 3. **Temporal Lobe and Frontal Lobe**

The function of the temporal lobe is to *remember* things or to *perceive*, whereas the function of the frontal lobe is to *think* of new things. The most prominent feature of humans in comparison to other animals, then, is their superior ability to think. Although all modern humans certainly have larger frontal lobes than do gorillas, mere size is not enough. The number of folds in the frontal lobe is also said to be crucial. These folds are formed by thinking in response to some stimulus. The average person is said to use only 18 percent of his brain capacity. He goes to the grave without ever using the remaining 82 percent. If true, this is a shame, and we should give some thought to using our frontal lobes more effectively. According to theory, a newborn human has 32 folds to its brain. Perhaps it is nothing but a bad pun, but in Japanese, the word for "fold" *(shiwa)* might be construed as the multiplied product of the words for "four" *(shi)* and "eight" *(wa)*: 4 × 8 = 32.

4

Stage Two: Basic Approaches to Improvement

I. Understand the Status Quo

The first problem in what we call improvement is to get a grip on the status quo. The most magnificent improvement scheme in the world will be worthless if your perception of the current situation is in error. We have a tendency to think that fictitious "facts" are real. I mean by this that either we do not try to grasp the real facts and simply hypothesize facts using guesswork, or we inadvertently ignore changes over time and assume that things are the same as they used to be — we ignore changes that occur over time. Too frequently, such mistakes lead us to confuse fictitious facts and real ones.

Even when we have recognized real facts, we must:

- Grasp facts in greater detail.
- Grasp facts quantitatively rather than qualitatively.
- Think in terms of categorical principles and understand phenomena by clearly classifying them.

To do this, we have to be able to analyze problems based on the "five elements of production:"

1. *Object*: what?
2. *Agent*: who?
3. *Method*: how?
4. *Space*: where?
5. *Time*: when?

Also, we must not forget to "observe from both sides," in terms of:

- *Process*: the course of changes in the object
- *Operation*: the course of changes in the agent

Finally, we cannot approach the real truth unless, rather than using our ordinary senses, we perceive in greater detail — using Frank B. Gilbreth's elements of motion, the 18 therbligs.

27

"Is" Outweighs "Ought"

We often say things such as, "It *ought* to be working according to the standard operation," or "It *ought* to be finished." Yet over and over again when we check to see what is really going on, it turns out that things are not necessarily going the way they are supposed to. "Ought" refers to *guesswork* and not to *fact*. We must recognize that although a guess may have a high probability of being correct, that still does not make it fact. For important matters, we must always grasp the real facts — i.e., what *is* — rather than what *ought* to be.

"Feel" Is Not Ideal

A lot of work done on the shop floor is carried out by "feel." "Feel" is a kind of experiential, statistical awareness that succeeds at a fairly high degree of probability. It follows that as we increase our reliance on a worker's feel for the job we get to a point where everything ends up being taken care of "by feel." Yet a feel for the job is ultimately vague; by its nature it cannot provide 100 percent reliability, and so sometimes, it is well off the mark. This is why I maintain that "feel" has to be on target three times in a row. Why are three tries needed? — A baseball pitcher has to get three strikes before he has done his job.

In plastic molding processes, maintaining suitable die temperatures is extremely important in stabilizing product quality. Yet D Plastics followed the following procedures:

1. Check temperature by placing a hand on the die.
2. Pinch the coolant line connected to the die to check flow rate by "feel."
3. Open and close the coolant line valve by "feel."

By switching to the following procedures, it became possible to eliminate chronic problems involving "whitening" of products:

1. Ascertain die temperature quantitatively by inserting thermometer into the die.
2. Fit a round plate to the valve and draw a scale on the plate so that the valve turns in increments of 1 degree Celsius.

In another operation at W Ceramics, plunger stroke size was determined by "feeling" the volume of glaze. This was changed so the stroke could be adjusted with a geared knob. A scale was drawn on the knob to allow quantitative control, and as a result, quality stabilized considerably, with previous off-specification rates of 30 percent dropping to less than 3 percent.

Relying on feel exaggerates the gap between skilled and unskilled workers, because while skilled workers can rapidly determine the proper conditions, unskilled workers can never get conditions stable. Quality can be stabilized however, when "feel" is abandoned in favor of quantitative measures.

There Is Truth Beyond Every Fact

We use the word *fact* to designate things we perceive, but in many cases our perception is only superficial. Oversights and misperceptions are revealed when we look deeper and observe more rigorously. It is only by means of such detailed, rigorous observation that we can begin to get a grip on truth. In matters of improvement, we begin by *grasping truth*.

You Don't Understand Not Understanding?

For a human being, not to understand "not understanding" is a problem without remedy. If we don't understand what it is that we don't understand, we have no idea what to do about it. In other words, we can't see something if we don't know to look for it. When people aren't aware of this possibility, they may end up unconsciously overlooking problems.

The first step toward solving a problem is to clarify what is not understood, i.e., to make a clear distinction between what we know and understand and what we do not know. By making this clear, we typically end up understanding about half of what was not known about the problem initially.

Next, the essence of what remains unknown is slowly revealed by the application of hypotheses and trials, until we can eventually arrive at a full understanding.

"More or Less" and the Facts of the Matter

Although we often speak of having "more or less" finished a job, I occasionally wonder just how much "more or less" really is.

At a company meeting, an employee used the phrase "more or less." One division head asked another one just how much "more or less" was, but the second was unable to give a clear reply because "more or less" was all that he had heard. Irritated at the thought of leaving things at that, he asked the first division head for specific figures, but he, too, could give only a vague reply because all he had heard were rough summaries. Like regimental commanders, the two were united by the limitations of their knowledge.

Hearing of the problem, the head of the manufacturing department appeared at the meeting, but things still were not cleared up, in spite of his contributions. Indeed, he ended up in the role of a brigade commander, alternately considering plans of action and making decisions. The plant manager, moreover, was like a division commander who did not know what was really going on.

Achieving a clear and quantitative grasp of the facts is quite a chore, which is why the way is always blocked by "company" level people who hesitate over what steps to take. Beyond them are the actual facts, and the "platoon" members who deal with them. If we don't begin by mastering the facts, discussions will always be on an ambiguous footing. No matter how long they last, they will tend to go around in circles and no real solutions will be found. [Editor's note: In Mr. Shingo's analogy, division, brigade, and regimental commanders are the three highest levels of "upper management" in the Japanese army. Companies and platoons correspond to shop-floor levels in management.]

Time Is Merely a Shadow of Motion

Supervisors frequently put pressure on plant workers to speed up their work, to get jobs done more quickly. Yet simply working faster — without improving the motions that take up the time — will not speed things up in the final analysis. Time is merely a shadow of motion, and no matter how much we may complain about shadows, nothing will happen unless we deal with the substance — motion — that throws the shadow.

Suppose a doctor visits a sick person and, taking his temperature, finds it to be above normal. Anybody would call the doctor an idiot if he were to cool off the thermometer and then announce to the patient that his temperature had dropped.

Yet the relationship between time and motion is analogous to the relationship between a thermometer and body temperature. Far too many supervisors complain about superficial time without improving the essential motions involved.

Motions are also influenced by operating conditions, which include five basic factors:

1. *Objects of production*: what?
2. *Agents of production*: who?
3. *Methods*: how?
4. *Space*: where?
5. *Time*: when?

In effect, then, if you want to speed things up, you must improve the underlying motions. And, if you want to improve those underlying motions, you must make thorough improvements in each of the elements on which they are based (objects and agents of production, methods, space, and time).

Accuracy and Precision Are Not the Same

Suppose one were to divide $1,000 among three people with an error of $10 or less. Under one *accurate* apportionment:

A gets $330
B gets $330
C gets $340

If we were to make a further division so that:

A gets $333
B gets $333
C gets $334

the distribution would still be accurate, but it would be more precise.

In the same way, even when degrees of precision differ, they are all accurate as long as they satisfy allowable tolerances. Consequently, it is a mistake to think that the more precise something is the more accurate it is. Frequently, rather than demand unnecessary precision, one need merely achieve a degree of accuracy that maintains the required degree of precision. Seeking more precision than necessary is often wasteful.

You Don't Need a Clock to Measure Time

We tend to believe that a clock is absolutely essential for measuring time. Yet according to Mr. N of Y Automotive Co., a clock is not always needed. Observation of workshop assembly lines reveals that processes that are always busy with work take more time and processes that are always waiting take less time.

Thus, without necessarily measuring time, it is possible to achieve overall balance and increase productivity by assigning work from the busy processes to the idle processes. Here, the measurement of time is a means, not an end, and if the goal is improvement, one need not assume that a clock is necessary to measure time.

"Various" and "Appropriate" Are Magic Words

On a visit to the R Record Company, I passed a process for inspecting disc masters and asked the department head who was showing me around what they were performing inspections for.

"For various things," he replied.

Since I had no idea what to make of that, I went to the worker who was actually doing the inspecting and asked him the same question. He, too, answered that he was inspecting "for various things."

This still did not tell me anything, so I pressed him to give me an example of what he meant. After a moment's thought, the inspection worker said, "Well, I'm checking to see whether or not the record grooves are clogged."

"I see," I replied. "Anything else?"

The worker thought about it some more and answered that he was checking to see if there were any scratches across the grooves.

"And are you inspecting for anything besides that?"

"Well, no." he said. "That's all."

When you came right down to it, "various things" referred to two items. Are we clearly cognizant of the facts when we talk about "various things"?

In my visits to production plants, I am often told that a phenomenon has various causes. When this happens, I insist that the causes be enumerated one by one and, strangely enough, workers on the shop floor usually can reel them off.

When "various" is followed by "appropriate," these change into magic words. Consider the following exchange:

"Why this stream of defects lately?"

"Well, you see, there are various reasons for that."

"So what are we going to do about it?"

"We'll think up appropriate measures...."

Or a similar conversation:

"We seem to be having a lot of equipment breakdown these days."

"Well, actually, there are various reasons for that."

"So what are we going to do about it?"

"I'll come up with appropriate measures."

How convenient when this ends the problem! "Various" and "appropriate" are truly magic, all-powerful words. They can be used at any time, anywhere, and in any situation. But in the final analysis, what is really solved by these words?

5

Basic Approaches to Improvement
II. The Pursuit of Goals

Improvement means the elimination of waste, and the most essential precondition for improvement is the proper pursuit of goals.

We must not be mistaken, first of all, about what improvement means. The four goals of improvement must be to make things:

- easier
- better
- faster
- cheaper

To achieve this, the pursuit of goals must be carried out thoroughly along three axes:

1. X: focus on the goals
2. Y: recognize multiple goals
3. Z: pursue goals systematically, working gradually toward higher-level or "underlying" goals

How thoroughly we pursue goals is affected by the quality of our improvement plans. This means, in any case, that it is impossible to be too thorough in pursuing underlying goals. Revolutionary improvement schemes can be developed by persistently tracking down these "source goals."

THE PURSUIT OF GOALS IN THREE DIMENSIONS

Eliminating waste means improving procedures that are too broadly or generally defined in terms of goals. It means asking *why* at every opportunity.

Just as grasping a physical object requires that it be seen in front, top, and side views, goals must be pursued along three dimensions, X, Y, and Z:

- *X*: focus your thinking
- *Y*: look for multiple goals
- *Z*: look for higher-level goals

Below are examples of the kinds of thinking needed.

Type X: Focus Your Thinking

At R Confectionery, in a process for melting the starch syrup base for caramel, 18 liter cans of syrup are placed in a heating oven. Its insufficient capacity could not keep up with production, however, and the company was looking around for a better way.

On a visit to the plant, I opened the doors of the oven and saw that the syrup cans were all overflowing and sticking to one another. Why, I asked, were the cans packed in so tightly? The official in charge of shop operations replied that they wanted to melt large quantities of syrup because of increased production and that recently, perhaps because of a change in the quality of the syrup, melting time had increased, so that they could only keep up by putting large quantities of syrup in the oven at the same time.

In response, I observed that heat can be transmitted in three ways — conduction, convection, or radiation — and that since the oven blew in hot air, it was essentially designed to heat by convection. Packing so many cans of syrup inside, however, meant that heat could only be transmitted by conduction. The cans in the center would therefore take longer to heat, and this resulted in longer heating times overall.

To remedy this, spaces were opened up to allow hot air to flow between cans, and a blower and an exhaust fan were installed to help the hot air circulate. As a result, per cycle capacity dropped to 60 percent, melting time was reduced by two-thirds — from 2 hours to 40 minutes. This meant a 180 percent net increase in melting capacity.

In this example, the key to improvement lay in following through with goal pursuit, by asking what was really involved in heating the syrup instead of assuming that all that was required was to pack in cans and blow in hot air.

Type Y: Look for Multiple Goals

The O Automobile plant was plagued by the problem of how to deal with electrodeposition coating liquid that was foaming and spilling out of a vat. The bubbles were eliminated when shop technicians sprayed an antifoaming agent on them, but this took a great deal of time and was costly. At a meeting on the subject, I asked a shop technician what a bubble was. He did not reply, but the look on his face told me he thought the answer was self-evident.

"Listen," I said to him, "a bubble is a pocket of air surrounded by a thin film of liquid coating material. I have the impression all of you have been trying to dissolve the coating enveloping the air, but couldn't you approach the problem just as well by simply removing the air inside?"

We went to the shop floor right away and I placed some foam in the palm of my hand. When I slapped my hand, the bubbles immediately disappeared. "The point here," I said, "is that all you have to do to destroy the bubbles is to apply some force."

When the foam was placed in the eccentric drainage tub of a washing machine and spun, it disappeared in 1 second and about 0.1 percent of the coating material flowed out.

In this case everyone assumed that the sole objective was to dissolve the film of coating material. The key to improvement lay in asking whether other objectives were involved. This led to the realization that all that was needed was to remove the air from within the bubbles. The problem was finally resolved by the simple act of forcing the bubbles through a screen.

Type Z: Look for Higher-Level Goals

A die casting plant carried out casting in three back-to-back shifts. The night-shift crews loaded items onto pallets and placed them in temporary storage areas, and the next day female part-time workers used presses to shear off sprue and flash. The sprue and flash on products meant that only a few fit on each pallet: a large pallet storage area was therefore required.

Since capacity would be tripled if the sprue and flash were eliminated, I asked why they could not be taken off during the night shift. The answer I was given was that this was not done because labor laws prohibited women from working at night.

"Then why not have men do it?"

"We can't make men work nights just for shearing."

"But there are already men working the night shift doing casting," I said. "Why not have them do the shearing in their spare time?"

We developed a method we called pre-machine pressing in which:

- The worker in charge of casting places the product on the lower die after cooling.
- The lower die enters the machine and the upper die descends and automatically shears off sprue and flash.
- Sprue and flash fall away and the product alone is dropped into a chute.

Thus, day and night, only the products are placed on pallets, cutting needed pallet storage space to one-third. This of course cuts pallet transport labor costs. In addition, processes are shortened since machine processing can begin immediately at the start of the morning shift.

We also realized that shearing would be easier if sprue and flash did not form randomly, but at specific sites. With this in mind, we set up air vents to collect air at specific locations, and this simplified processing even further.

We then asked two questions:

- Why does flash form?
- Why are air vents needed?

The answers we came up with were:

- Flash forms because there is air inside the dies.
- Gasses form inside the liquid metal.

In the end, we were able to eliminate flash and air vents altogether by adopting a vacuum-forming method. A vacuum pump removes air inside the die once the die is tightened, and gas that has seeped into the liquid metal is sucked out. Although it is true that gates and channels remain, it is possible that these too can be eliminated by adopting the "hot runner" and "pin gate" concepts used in resin molding.

Thus, we see a progression:

- Shearing must be performed by women during the day.

- Shearing can also be performed at night.
- Flash is eliminated by using air vents.
- Flash and air vents become unnecessary.

Higher-order levels of improvement can be achieved by pursuing — and developing techniques that correspond to — objectives at higher and higher levels.

X — FOCUS

What Does the Boiler Want?

In my student days I heard a story about Tsunekichi Takuma, the inventor of the Takuma boiler.

Takuma was born in Kishū, some 90 kilometers south of Osaka, and inherited the work of logging on family land in the second and third decades of this century. The round saws used for cutting lumber at that time were powered by steam, thus creating a demand for a small, efficient boiler. The holder of the patent for an appropriate boiler lived in Osaka, and he came to Takuma seeking financial support for practical trials of his invention. Funds were provided repeatedly, but a practical boiler never appeared. Rather than continue the loan, Takuma asked for, and received, the patent rights to the boiler, which, the inventor explained, was on the verge of success. Takuma tried the device but it still would not work. He tested countless approaches; the costs of his experiments used up the family fortune, and unrepaid debts to family and friends mounted. At length, no longer able to stay in his home town, Takuma moved to Osaka but remained obsessed with the invention.

In time, his research reached its goal, but Takuma found himself with no money to test the version he was sure would work. Recalling that a friend of his from elementary school days was now running a large business in Seoul, Korea, Takuma decided to ask him for financial support.

Takuma scraped up money for the trip and left Osaka for Shimonoseki, at the western tip of Honshū. From there he took the ferry bound for Pusan. Before daybreak, Takuma stood on the deck, deep in thought.

"I'm sure I'll succeed this time," he thought, "but I've failed before when I'd been confident that things would go well. There's no 100 percent guarantee that this time will be a success. Maybe I can get the loan if I go to Seoul, but if I fail, I'll default again, because I'll never be able to repay it. On the other hand, if I were to jump into the sea by way of apology to my family and my friends, they would probably manage all right." Cowardice overcame him and he put his foot up on the railing to jump in.

At that very moment, however, the sun rose from the east in a burst of light and the sparkling waves dazzled his eyes. A voice came to him from the heavens and asked him a question: "Takuma! You seem to want so much to invent this boiler — have you ever asked the boiler what it is it wants done?"

The instant Takuma heard this, he realized that he had in fact never asked the boiler what it wanted. He turned toward the sky and asked the boiler, "What do you want?" .Again a voice rolled down from the heavens with the answer: "Good water circulation."

An idea for the most critical part of the Takuma boiler came to him then and he gave up the notion of dying. Disembarking at Pusan, he purchased a small grill for frying salt, conducted some experiments with it, and hit on an idea for the boiler's core mechanism. He went to Seoul, managed to borrow the money, and returned to Osaka. There, he conducted further experiments and trial runs and, with one success on the heels of another, he produced the most efficient boiler in the world, the Takuma boiler.

The English B & W boiler was reputed to be the most efficient, but in that boiler, bubbles of steam collect in the water pipes and block circulation. Takuma boilers, on the other hand, have double pipes: steam rises in the outer pipes while cooling water falls in the inner pipes to allow smooth circulation of steam and water.

The story was told with much joking and punning, and when I heard it, I did not take it too seriously. But in visits to factories later on, I realized, indeed, that we have to be able to hear what our machines are telling us; difficulties will naturally make themselves clear when we fix our undivided attention on the task at hand. We begin to hear what our machines are really saying only by doggedly pursuing the ultimate purpose of the task, and by asking "why" over and over again.

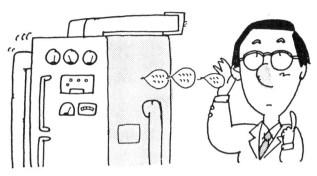

Listen to the machine

Listen to the Machine

Frequently we view industrial plants, as though we were riding around on a tour bus. This is not good. It is important to stop at the first machine and observe it for a minimum of thirty minutes. Even when we watch a machine that is not thought to have any problems, the machine itself will tell us before long which parts to fix and where it is not performing well.

Moreover, standing in front of a machine that is thought to be problem-free is essential for identifying waste. Just as important is tracking down the goals of individual tasks by constantly asking "why?" Indeed, this must have been precisely what was going through Tsunekichi Takuma's mind on the sea near Shimonoseki when he turned toward the heavens and asked what the boiler wanted.

When many machines are involved, it is effective to distinguish operations according to their characteristics and then deal with representative operations. Thus, by taking the time to observe typical operations, e.g., the machining of shafts, faceplates, and tubes on lathes, one can better understand and more quickly identify problems in other similar operations.

Once at a facility manufacturing high-pressure hoses, Mr. Sakamoto, a department head, told me that steel wire wrapped around the hose tended to sever and that they were troubled by the long time it took to repair the damage. "What should we do," he asked me, "to cut the repair time?"

"Mr. Sakamoto," I said, "all you need is to keep the steel wire from being cut. That means you just ask the machine why the wire gets cut."

"Ask the machine? But what should I do?"

I replied that the machine would speak naturally if he were to stand in front of it for at least half a day and observe its movements carefully.

Mr. Sakamoto did stand in front of the machine for half a day and observe its movements. When the steel wire was cut, he looked hard to see why it was cut and saw what was happening. He noticed that, to wind the steel wire around the hose, 16 wires were fed through a comb-shaped guide and that there were two places on the guide where the wire was bent at right angles. Streamlined grooves running along the flow of wire through the guide were substituted for this arrangement, and thereafter not a single wire was cut.

From that time on, whenever a problem came up, Mr. Sakamoto said he made a point to stand in front of the machine and listen to what it had to say.

Why Grease Scrap Metal?

Once at an IE workshop I directed the following question to a participant sitting in the front row, a department head who had 25 years of experience with presses.

"Tell me, Mr. S, in forming with progressive dies, why do you grease the surface of hoop stock?

"It's because you need lubrication when the pressure is applied," he answered.

"I see. I understand that you need grease on the parts to which pressure is applied, but why on earth do you grease the scrap metal that doesn't come in contact with the press?"

"Well, you see, greasing the scrap just happens naturally because it's attached."

"Is it perhaps because you can sell the scrap for more if it has been greased?" I asked.

Mr. S vigorously denied that suggestion; so I continued, "If greasing scrap is an utter waste, then we have no business saying we do it because it's attached, do we?"

In the end, greased scrap was eliminated by spraying grease

from the top and bottom dies used in the pressing process. Mr. S reported that although he had worked with presses for 25 years, that was the first time anyone had ever asked him why he was greasing scrap metal.

Paint the Air?

The S Fountain Pen Company's T plant is located in the countryside and surrounded by rice paddies. Waste from the painting booth consequently needs to be treated, but during periods of heavy rainfall, the paddies used to be contaminated by overflows of polluted water from the water treatment facilities. This provoked frequent complaints from neighboring farmers and each year the firm was paying out substantial sums to compensate them.

At this point, the company decided to conduct a fact-finding survey of the plant. The survey revealed that in the painting booth, pigment was sprayed onto 50 fountain pen caps, inserted on pins mounted on top of a revolving stand. Excess pigment was led off to a water screen and flushed to the bottom of the booth. From there it flowed into a waste treatment device where it was neutralized; drainage canals then took the purified water outside the plant. This meant that the least error in treatment could result in contaminated water being sent into nearby paddies.

When I asked the plant manager what the operation was for, he made a rather strange face — as though the answer were obvious — and replied that it was for painting fountain pen caps.

"That's right," I said, "but isn't it true that more than 50 percent of the paint is painting the air?"

"Painting the air? Well, I suppose you might say that, but...."

"Look," I told him. "If all you have to do is paint the caps, why paint the air as well? Isn't there some painting method that would allow you to paint only the caps?" The manager thought about this, and when I visited the plant the next day a greatly improved process was already in place:

- An extremely small painting booth was constructed.
- The pen caps were supported by rotating rods, so that the caps could turn.
- A special sprayer was built with a nozzle that blew out only extremely small amounts of pigment. This nozzle was designed

to move up and down automatically. It therefore painted only
the caps and sprayed out almost no excess pigment.
- Five such sprayers were installed in a row so that painting
could be done in groups of five.
- Exhaust air from the small painting booth was sucked out,
and the entire unit was constructed so that such exhaust was
extremely localized. In addition, a sponge-like urethane rubber filtering device attached to the exhaust channel absorbed
all excess pigment.
- Urethane rubber that had absorbed pigment was replaced
every day and incinerated.

As a result of these changes, no contaminated water whatsoever
left the plant. Farmers from the surrounding region to whom the
new setup was shown agreed that improvement had taken place and
released the company thereafter from the payment of compensation.

It was moving to hear the plant manager describe the profound
relief he felt. "Until recently," he said, "I always used to worry
when it rained hard that contaminated water was leaving the plant.
These changes have really helped, though, and now I don't have
those worries."

Even so, many Japanese plants continue to "paint the air" in
painting booths. What is more, technicians frequently do not even
notice that anything is wrong.

"Drying the Glue" Means Just What It Says

In a procedure used to build television cabinets, boards were
joined to one another with glue and then dried. This used to take a
long time, because the joined boards were placed in a drying oven
and dried from the outside. The improvements below cut drying
time in half:

- The matched surfaces of the boards are heated beforehand.
- After glue is spread on and the boards are joined, they are
placed in the drying oven.

The heat held by the boards allows the solvent in the glue to evaporate more rapidly. Indeed, "drying the glue" involves two things —
evaporating the solvent, and chemical changes (i.e., polymerization)
in the glue itself.

Both for evaporating the solvent and for polymerization, it turned out to be more effective to heat the glue directly than to heat it through the boards from the outside.

Is Drilling Really the Best Way to Make Holes?

In many hole-boring operations a bit cuts through the entire hole section. For large diameter holes, moreover, a small guide hole is often drilled in the center and then a larger bit widens the hole.

Processing time can be reduced if a cutter with a cylindrical tip matching the hole diameter is used to cut out the circumference of the hole. The cutout pieces can also be put to other uses. Clearly, rather than drilling an entire hole, it is sufficient merely to cut away the hole's circumference.

Do We Really Cut Things with a Lathe?

After delivering a lecture at Citroen in France, I retired to an antechamber and thanked Miss Junko Ishii, my interpreter.

"Not at all!" she replied. "The interpreting part isn't that difficult; what's really draining is when there are gaps in the language."

"Gaps in the language?" I asked. "What do you mean?"

"For example, in your talk today, you used the phrase, 'cut things with a lathe.' But in French you can't use an expression like that."

"Why not?" I asked in surprise. "Nothing could be more natural than to cut things with a lathe."

"It doesn't work that way. You have to say that you mount tools on the lathe and then cut things with the tools. Since a lathe is simply a machine for turning things you attach to it, you can't actually cut things with just a lathe. Japanese has many gaps like this that can't be interpreted just as they are. You've got to think carefully about what they mean."

When I thought about it, I realized — and I still feel — that there are many such gaps in the way we express ourselves and that we frequently do not notice them.

After returning to Japan, I visited an electric company that had a problem of "lead wires coming out."

When I asked what that meant, I was told that after several lead wires were twisted together and soldered, vinyl caps were put on and fused with a soldering iron. It turned out that some of the wires would come loose due to vibration when they were transported by conveyor. Although, ideally, the vinyl caps should harden rapidly, in fact the process took a little time and this was why the wires were coming out.

"So all you have to do is cool the vinyl caps so that they harden quickly," I said.

"No, we're already doing that. We're using a fan to cool them, but the cooling is still too slow."

At this point I went to the shop floor to observe the operation and saw how they were cooling the caps with a fan.

"Tell me, Mr. M," I asked, "just what are you doing?"

"What do you mean? I'm cooling these vinyl caps with a fan."

"But surely you can't cool the vinyl caps with a fan," I said.

"Certainly we can," the worker replied. "They cool down, all right. The problem is that they take too long to cool."

"What I'm trying to say is that you can't cool them with a fan. What's really cooling them isn't the force of the breeze from the fan at all, is it?"

"Oh, well, I suppose not."

"The breeze from the fan is zero at the center of the blades and radiates out at the circumference. Your current technique is inefficient because only minimal air strikes the vinyl caps. It would work better if you were to concentrate the air coming from the fan and construct a guide to make it strike the caps directly. The caps could be cooled if the air were focused on them for a longer period of time.

The implementation of this improvement speeded cooling, and defects involving detached wires completely disappeared (see Figure 4).

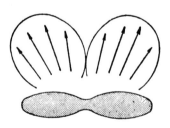

FIGURE 4. **Air From the Blades of a Fan**

As a matter of interest, we might ask whether our linguistic gaps are accompanied by more basic gaps in consciousness. If such gaps do exist, they will tend to cause problems.

Why Not Make It Winter All the Time?

This example involves heaters for hot plates. Nichrome wire was inserted in a pipe and powder was sealed in to insulate the circumference. To eliminate water of crystallization within the powder, the assembly was heated at high temperature in an oven and then cooled. At this point problems arose when the unit absorbed moisture from the atmosphere, making the insulation less effective.

I visited the plant to observe the operation. There, Mr. Yai, the department head, told me that although quality was good during the winter when atmospheric humidity was low, high humidity during the summer resulted in inferior insulation. "I wish," Mr. Yai said, "that it were winter all the time."

I thought about this for a while and then turned to Mr. Yai. "Look," I said. "You may want it to be winter all the time, but there's nothing we can do about the seasons. If, on the other hand, we're only talking about the desirability of winter conditions while heaters are cooling, then all we have to do is use an enclosure filled with low-humidity air."

In looking around for low-humidity air, we learned that compressed air was most appropriate, and so after the heating stage, compressed air was pumped in for the cooling operation. This method made it possible to produce items with extremely effective insulating properties.

Now I will cite the opposite case, in which S Printing wanted it to be summer all the time.

In the printing process, water was applied to repel ink from places where it was not wanted on the letterpress. Low humidity in winter caused the roller that supplied this water to dry out rapidly, resulting in inadvertent smudges on the press. In this case, the head of the manufacturing department wanted it to be summer all the time.

I visited the shop and suggested that the water supply roller be enclosed by a vinyl curtain, inside which the humidity could be monitored and water supplied as needed. This change reduced the occurrence of smudges considerably.

Here again, all that was necessary was to ensure that "summer" conditions always prevailed around the water supply rollers. Thus, even where it appears that natural phenomena cannot be altered, focusing on the real problem can reveal surprisingly effective improvements.

High-Diversity, Low-Volume Production Is Not a Big Deal

When people treat high-diversity, low-volume production as a "big deal," they should realize that this sort of thinking is, in itself, a problem. High-diversity, low-volume production seems like a big deal because many kinds of products are made in small lots. A production plant is a place where things are made, however, so consequently the real problem is the many different ways there are to make things.

Machines carry out only a limited number of functions:

- A drill press bores holes.
- A lathe cuts the circumferences of cylindrical items, machines surfaces, and bores holes.
- A milling machine machines surfaces and cuts grooves.
- A press punches holes, and bends, squeezes, and stamps metal, plastic, wood, or other materials.

At S Manufacturing, which makes resistors, I asked what problems had been encountered. I received this succinct response from the company president: "High-diversity, low-volume production."

"Really?" I said. "I heard that you made nothing but resistors. Am I wrong? Are you making cars? Televisions? Motors?"

"No," he replied, "we only make resistors, but there are many different kinds."

"Do you mean that some are round and some are octagonal and some are triangular?"

"No, no. They're all rectangular, but, you see, there are all different sizes."

"Listen," I said. "These differences in product size may certainly cause some difficulty for your people in design and parts purchasing. The problem for people in the plant, though, is how many ways there are to make the products. I want you to tell me all the methods you use to make resistors, including operations that you perform only once every three years."

We had the foremen tell us the different types of operations and I arranged the results in descending order of frequency. I graphed the totals on a curve and we found that out of 36 types of operations, 75 percent were of five types:

1. drilling
2. tightening screws
3. soldering
4. connecting wires
5. deburring

For *drilling*, we decided to use a multi-axis drill. Even though the company had already purchased such a device, no one liked to use it because, as I discovered, setup changes were thought to be too difficult. I introduced them to the concept of SMED and we made it possible to complete changeovers in five minutes. The subsequent use of the multi-axis drill vastly improved efficiency.

In *tightening screws*, efficiency was greatly improved through the use of a screw setter, a tool that automatically fed screws to the tip of the driver.

Active improvements were also instituted for *soldering*, *connecting wires*, and *deburring*, and production doubled within three months.

Thus, to improve high-diversity, low-volume production, it is extremely important to think just in terms of operations and not to be led astray by the various external appearances of things. Secondly, using SMED is extremely effective for dealing with the problem of long setup times. If setups can be cut from four hours to three minutes, the greatest obstacle to high-diversity, low-volume production is significantly reduced.

In any case, rather than vaguely assuming that high-diversity, low-volume production is a big deal, if one asks doggedly what the real difficulties of such production are, ways to handle the problem will reveal themselves to a surprising extent. High-diversity, low-volume production is, at most, a "middling deal."

Most Oil Used in Machining Is Wasted

Go to any machine shop and you will see oil poured on during machining. Why, one might ask, do we apply oil while machining? The answer will probably be something to the effect that putting on oil is necessary. Why is it necessary? We are usually told that the oil is needed for lubrication.

However, if we think about what functions are served by the presence of oil during machining, we find it serves three functions:

1. Cooling blades
2. Removing the buildup of cuttings on blades
3. Lubricating cutting surfaces

The relative importance of each of these functions is roughly:

- Blade cooling — 50 percent
- Blade cleaning — 30 percent
- Lubricating cutting surfaces — 20 percent

The friction on blades during machining generates high temperatures that rob the blades of their temper; sharpness falls off because they lose hardness. Rapid cooling is therefore required, but applying oil only absorbs heat through conduction. A better approach is to apply oil mist so that latent heat is drawn off by evaporation. In the case of water, the difference is staggering:

- One calorie is sufficient to lower the temperature of 1 cc of water by 1 degree Celsius via conduction.
- Eighty calories are needed to vaporize one cc of water.

This is what we call "magic cutting." It will necessarily reduce the amount of oil used by more than 90 percent.

Another effect of this approach is that cuttings on blades are cleaned away because blades are sprayed at high pressures. In particular, cuttings frequently clog blades or blade grooves in so-called magic tapping, but when cutting is completed and "magic-cutting" oil is sprayed on as the tap is withdrawn, products are both cleaned and cooled. This not only produces clean threads, it greatly lessens the incidence of worn and broken taps and their lives can generally be doubled. This is because tap breakage results from excessive resistance due to cuttings that accumulate between blades and in blade grooves. Furthermore, since friction increases significantly when cuttings come between the product and the blade cutting surfaces, it is extremely effective to remove such cuttings beforehand.

I once heard that the Y plant could not find a way to bore long straight holes for rifle barrels. They did not achieve success until they bored a small hole down the center of the drill bit and injected oil at high pressure so that the cuttings were pushed along the bit grooves and washed away.

The next issue is how to provide oil for lubricating cutting surfaces. This function requires far less oil than the previous two. One example comes from F Electric, where, in a broaching operation, large quantities of oil used to be poured on from above. Instead, after the broach had cut downward through the product, an oil mist was sprayed upward in conformity with the angle of the blades. This both cooled the metal and removed cuttings with the result that blade temper improved. It meant, too, that there was no obstacle to using the oil remaining on the broach as the sole cutting surface lubricant. Along with boosting production, this led to an increase in broach life of over 50 percent and a 90 percent reduction in oil consumption.

When an oil mist is used, appropriate measures must be taken to deal with the smoke generated by evaporation. In general, installing a simple antismoke device around the cutting site is sufficient.

When we look closely at the application of large quantities of oil in machining — in terms of the functions of machine oil — we discover that some 90 percent of such oil is wasted.

What Is Lighting For?

The small city of Boulder, Colorado, lies at the foot of the Rocky Mountains near the city of Denver. The air is clean in Boulder, and the scenery is spectacular.

On the 24th and 25th of April in 1985, I visited the Granville-Phillips Company in Boulder as a consultant on improvement. The president of the firm, Mr. Daniel G. Bills, is extremely enthusiastic about improvement; he told me he had participated in a November 1984 study mission to Japan and had heard me speak in Tokyo.

After returning to America, Mr. Bills immediately put Japanese management methods into effect. As a result, profitability in the first six months rose 260 percent over the previous six months.

During the first morning of my two-day visit, I presented concepts of improvement and production management improvement to an audience of about 150 people that included the nearly 100 employees of Granville-Phillips, top members of the local Chamber of Commerce, university professors, and city officials. That afternoon, I visited the plant to observe operations and made suggestions for improvement.

Granville-Phillips produces vacuum control devices. These products contain printed circuit boards and some operations involve inserting items such as diodes and resistors into these boards.

As is true in most American plants, the workplace is pleasant — neat and much better lit than in Japan. Yet sometimes workers made mistakes in inserting items into circuit boards. A shop manager wanted to know how to eliminate such defects. I remarked that the plant was brightly lit and asked the manager the purpose of lighting the workplace. She replied that if it were dark, workers could not distinguish among the various products and parts. "We've provided ample lighting," she said, "because workers have to insert the pins on resistors into tiny holes on the circuit boards."

"It's true," I replied, "that if it were too dark, it might be difficult to tell parts from one another; that requires a certain level of light. If what you're really doing is inserting parts into circuit boards, however, then to me the most important thing is that the holes on the circuit boards be clearly visible.

"What you want to do, then, is to decrease the light from above slightly and illuminate the boards from below. That should make the holes in the circuit boards easier to locate."

I had this idea tested immediately and the new lighting scheme made the holes far easier to distinguish. It also made it possible to determine at a glance whether any parts had been inadvertently left off a board. The rate of insertion errors subsequently fell to zero. By using illumination masks corresponding to the parts needed for each particular process, insertion errors were totally eliminated. Overhead illumination had been increased in response to poor hole visibility, but in fact this produced distracting reflections. It turned out to be far more effective to lower overhead illumination and provide more light from below.

Thus, rather than simply assuming that more illumination is better, it is preferable to consider what the *point* of illumination is and then devise lighting that responds to the real goals of the task at hand.

Speed Alone Isn't Enough

When I graduated from school in 1930, Dr. Sugiyama, my physics professor, addressed the students: "You are all about to leave this school and go out into the world," he said. "When you do, remember not to concentrate merely on speed. What you've got to pay attention to is velocity. No matter what record-breaking speeds you may be able to attain as you swim along, you will never reach your goals unless you are moving in specific directions toward specific objectives.

"Speed is fine as far as it goes, but velocity requires a direction component. So as you're swimming, you've got to raise your heads from time to time and check to make sure you're moving toward your objectives."

Unless you are heading straight for your objectives, the most heroic efforts in the world will only be as effective as the component of work directly related to your goals. Indeed, when carrying out improvements, you will only be truly effective when you first set your objectives and then head straight for them.

NC Machines Can Measure Precisely

Numerical control (NC) machines are considered to possess an extremely high degree of processing precision because of their high degree of mechanical precision.

Yet isn't the truly distinguishing characteristic of NC machines their *measuring* precision?

Suppose it is essential that movement of 100 mm $+/-0$ must be attained in feeding even a rickety lathe. A problem arises, does it not, if that distance cannot be shown both accurately and precisely?

An actual example of this situation comes from Z Industries. On a double sizer for cutting matching panels, the installation of a magnascale — a highly precise measuring device — made it possible to read off blade position both accurately and precisely, and this in turn made possible a striking improvement in the dimensional precision of the final products.

A Tag Is a Tool for Transporting Intentions

A tag is said to be a tool that transports intentions through space, whereas a register is a tool that transports intentions in time. It follows, then, that tags can be eliminated by bringing the senders and receivers of intentions closer to one another, and registers can be eliminated by reducing the time involved in transmitting intentions — that is, by taking *immediate action*.

Time Is Not the Same as Timing

We frequently say that something didn't get done on time. We probably ought to say that it didn't get done with proper timing.

I once saw a newspaper advertisement in which S Electric claimed it produced "a television a minute." How could a television be produced in one minute, I wondered. What the ad meant, of course, was that one minute was the time between the completion of the one television set and the completion of the next, not that the television production process took one minute. The assembly of a television from start to finish might take four hours, but the space between television no. 1 and television no. 2 was one minute.

We see, then, that *time* and *timing* mean completely different things. Clocks, for example, possess different modes of expression. *Digital clocks* accurately express timing, whereas *analog clocks* help us gain an intuitive grasp of time. In the same way, the difference between time problems and timing problems must be understood in production. For example, delays are less a matter of time and more the effect of timing.

For example, one of the jobs at T Industries involved preheating mandrels used in insulated tubing. Where 40 tubes per hour had been produced in the past, the idea now was to increase this to 60 tubes per hour. The problem was the capacity of the oven for heating the mandrels — it would only hold 40.

I decided to visit the plant and observe the operation. Sure enough, the oven could hold only 40 mandrels. But as I watched the job being performed, I saw that they would use half the total number of mandrels — about 20 — and then feed new mandrels into the oven. When they used the remaining 20 mandrels, another group of new mandrels was supplied. At this point I talked to the workers.

"With the method you're using now," I said, "the newly supplied mandrels can be used for a heating time corresponding to the time that 20 tubes are used, i.e., 1.5 minutes × 20 minutes = 30 minutes. This means that if you increase production to 60 tubes per hour, what you have to do is to divide the oven into four and use ten mandrels at a time, so that ten new mandrels are supplied whenever there is a vacancy. This is because mandrels are used now at one-minute intervals, so that while 30 preheated ones are being used, the ten new mandrels are being preheated.

"In any event, your wanting one tube per minute means that you want an interval of one minute to separate the first tube and the second tube. It's a question of *timing*.

How long a mandrel is heated before it reaches a suitable temperature is a question of *time*. Since each mandrel needs to be heated for 30 minutes, reducing the feed units will cut down on the amount of space needed. If the units are lined up and fed successively from one side to the other, the total time it takes them to go through need be only 30 minutes. That would mean you could get by with even less space."

The outcome, then, was that the job could be done with an oven whose capacity was only 40 mandrels. Here, once again, the key to solving the problem lay in distinguishing between timing — or the number of items required — and time — which referred to the question of heating.

Y — MULTIPLE GOALS

Presses Have Only Four Functions

"I'd like to make production more rational," President K of T Ironworks once told me, "but it's awfully hard to do when you're dealing with high diversity and low volume."

"Look," I replied, "your plant does pressing, right? Tell me, just what sort of work is it that presses perform?"

"They do various things."

"What do you mean by that?"

"I mean that we have many types of products, so the presses do various things!"

"That's not what I mean," I said. "No matter how many different products are involved, the work that a press itself carries out is probably restricted to things like punching holes, bending, and squeezing."

"I see," he said. "The press itself does only three things. No, there's one more. It's flattening."

"All right, then. Even with that, you're dealing with only four items. And then after a product has been worked on by a press, it either falls out, stays in the lower die, or remains attached to the upper die. There are only three possibilities, right?"

Then I continued, "You think the job is so awfully hard because you are blinded by the large number of products you work with. But you haven't stopped to think about how many different types of work the presses themselves do."

I had him divide his plants' manufacturing processes into types, and for the main process types, presses were positioned according to process flow. For each of a number of types of processes, an 80 cm-wide conveyor belt was set up down the middle and 12 presses were arranged on either side. A one-piece flow was then established by linking the process via this central conveyor. This easily permitted the reorganization of high-diversity, low-volume production into one-piece flow operations. Half a year later, production had been considerably streamlined:

- Productivity — up 100 percent
- Production period — reduced 90 percent
- Work-in-process — reduced 90 percent
- Defect rate — reduced 87.5 percent

Do Punches Break Because They Are Weak?

During one of my visits to the M Company, the head of the press department told me he had been having problems with punches breaking and asked if there were a way to take care of the problem. When I asked him why the punches broke, he suggested it was because the material they were made of was weak.

"That's odd," I said. "If the material were weak, then the punches wouldn't be able to make holes.

"Punches work because they are made of harder material than the sheet material they cut through. Because they are brittle, though, they are susceptible to buckling. Typically, we fit urethane rubber bushings onto punches to improve extraction. We restrain the metal sheet and punch the hole, then hold down the sheet with urethane rubber and withdraw the punch. This improves extraction of the punch, but it does not prevent buckling."

At this point, we fitted a steel bushing onto the bottom half of the punch to keep it from buckling and then breaking. On the top half, we fitted the urethane rubber bushing to improve punch extraction. As a result, no matter how worn punches became, they never broke.

Forming and Achieving Precision Are Different Functions

A form cutter was used to machine mounting blocks for turbine blades. The operation took a long time and since form cutters are expensive and wear out quickly, repeated grinding was unavoidable.

"Machining a mounting block," I said to the head of the department, "requires the performance of two functions — forming and achieving precision. As far as forming is concerned, why not drill several holes with a boring machine and then *grind* them to the proper shape? Precision can be achieved by using the form cutter only at the last stage of the operation."

Putting this suggestion into effect reduced costs considerably; the operation time was cut by 75 percent and cutter life was extended fivefold (see Figure 5).

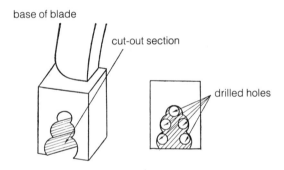

FIGURE 5. **Turbine Blade Processing**

What Do Polishing Machines Do?

Z Machinery is a machine tool manufacturer whose polishing machines were always busy. Six polishing machines running overtime could not get the job done, so the firm was about to buy another machine.

This was how things stood when I visited the factory to observe operations. The foreman explained that the polishing stone moves across a surface eleven times to polish it. I then asked the head of the shop unit to tell me just what it was that a polishing machine did. He gave me a puzzled look and told me that a polishing machine was for polishing.

"Look," I said, "a polishing machine performs two very different tasks. The first is grinding. In this instance, since an ordinary blade will not stand up to a surface that has been hardened by tempering or by rapid cooling, machining must be done with hard carborundum blades.

"The second task is polishing. This involves giving a mirrorlike finish to surfaces that milling machines or other machines in prior processes have left rough. What you're doing here is cleaning up rough surfaces. That means your goal is polishing. If all you're doing is cleaning up the cuts made by a milling machine, then why do you need eleven passes of the stone?

"Now then," I continued. "I want you to find out for me how much your milling machine is currently leaving to be polished."

The worker checked right away and found that the milling machine was leaving between 0.6 mm and 0.9 mm of material to be polished down.

If the polishing operation really consisted of grinding away the rough surfaces left by a cutter, then the next question was how much leeway the cutter required. I asked the worker to install a gauge that could measure with greater precision the cutting margin remaining after a cut had been made by the milling machine.

By the next time I visited the plant, a 0.09 mm margin had been found to be sufficient, so the gauge was used to ensure that the milling machine cut just that far. Now the job could be done with three passes of the stone, and this reduced the number of polishing machines used from six to two. In addition, it was, of course, no longer necessary to run the machines overtime.

In the final analysis, the milling operation had been on the safe side, cutting conservatively to avoid defects from overcuts. This increased the amount of material that had to be polished. Through the use of a precise measurement device, however, the material to be ground away was minimized, and it became possible to reduce drastically the number of passes made by polishing stones. Certainly, a solution would have been discovered sooner had a sustained effort been made to identify the true purpose of the polishing machines.

Here again, it's safe to say that the problem was insufficient precision in measurement rather than inadequate machining capacity.

Engraving and Oil Removal

In this operation, labels such as "magnification" and "lens performance" were engraved on the hoods of optical machinery. Since cutting oil was used in the course of engraving, subsequent plating could not be carried out unless triclene was used to remove the excess oil.

Manufacturing Department A, on the first floor, had oil-removal apparatus, so it was asked to carry out the job. Because the department had its own tasks to perform, however, oil removal always ended up on the back burner, becoming the source of troublesome delays. This, in turn, caused difficulties for Manufacturing Department D, the site of the operation on the fourth floor.

The people in Manufacturing Department D were in a quandary: When they asked the plant manager for oil-removal apparatus of their own, the request was flatly denied. The low volume of work involved, said the manager, simply did not justify specialized and expensive oil-removal equipment. "Why not have Manufacturing Department A do it for you the way it does now?"

When I decided to visit the engraving workshop, the department head was investigating the possibility of a compact, inexpensive oil-removal device. In the operation, cutting oil was poured on while the magnification, name, and other labels were engraved by a machine equipped with a profiling apparatus. After observing this, I turned to the department head and told him that I had come up with a satisfactory solution to the problem.

"A solution?" he exclaimed. "What is it?"

"All you have to do," I said, "is to eliminate the use of cutting oil."

"No oil? That won't work. You've got to have cutting oil to do machining."

I then asked him why oil was necessary.

"You use cutting oil for cutting. It's just common knowledge, isn't it?"

"And what does that mean," I asked, "that it's common knowledge?"

The department head fell silent.

"There are three reasons for using cutting oil," I explained.

"The first is to cool the blades. Temperatures rise because cutting generates heat, and higher temperatures affect the hardness of cutting tools. The primary effect of using cutting oil is to prevent this. This effect probably accounts for 50 percent of the use of cutting oil.

"The second reason is to remove cuttings. Shavings that adhere to cutting blades reduce sharpness and increase heat buildup, so they must be removed. Especially when you are cutting threads with a tap: the complete removal of cuttings between blades and between grooves in the tap will improve the cut of the thread and can increase tap life by 50 percent or so. This accounts for another 30 percent of the use of cutting oil.

"The third reason lies in the lubricating effect, which reduces friction during cutting. I think we can say that this accounts for the remaining 20 percent of oil use.

"Although it is generally thought that 100 percent of the reason for using cutting oil is lubrication, this is a mistake. The most important use of cutting oil is to cool the blades.

"If cooling is the most important reason for using cutting oil, then one is not obliged to use *oil* at all. For the sort of light cutting involved in engraving, why not come up with some other method of cooling — for example, simply lowering the temperature of the air?"

Rather than using oil, then, I suggested blowing compressed air on the blades. People on the shop floor strongly opposed this idea, saying it would shorten engraving blade life, but they allowed us to go ahead and test the method anyway. When we actually used compressed air, we found that it was sufficient to cool the blades. The principle effect was that all cuttings were blown away so that scrap from the cutting operation did not interfere with the tool. Along with minimizing wear and actually extending blade life by some 30 percent, this made it possible to produce extremely clean engravings.

Naturally, the need for oil removal was also eliminated, and this eliminated the problem of delays.

A majority of technicians at many plants still believe that "common knowledge" dictates the use of cutting oil when machining. It appears that objectives are not being thoroughly examined — that people are not questioning their goals. Why is this?

Steam Is Composed of Moisture and Heat

At a tea processing plant, steam is used to cook tea leaves. The leaves are more or less tough depending on the grade of tea, however, so the quantity of steam needs to be regulated accordingly.

Tea quality is determined by three factors: taste, aroma, and color. The considerable steaming required for tough-leaved Grade 3 teas, though, tends to wash away each of these attributes. There is a subtle knack involved in balancing the demands of tenderness against taste, aroma, and color, and the steaming operation calls for a great deal of skill.

What it came down to was that when high-temperature steaming was attempted, the increased moisture washed out taste, aroma, and color. This was the situation when I addressed myself to Mr. Horiuchi, a master teamaker.

"Let's think about what steaming means. The process is composed, is it not, of two parts: supplying moisture and supplying heat? The temperature has to be raised when the tea leaves are tough, right? But the way you are doing things now, you are adding more moisture than is necessary just so that you can apply large quantities of steam. Why not introduce moisture and heat separately?"

Following this suggestion, the plant adopted a method in which moisture is added in the form of mist, and heat is supplied in the form of hot air. This reduced the level of skill necessary to perform the operation and at the same time made it possible to produce tea of extremely high quality.

"Liquefaction" Involves More than Just Melting Ingots

When I once asked the head of a manufacturing department what liquefaction was, he replied that it meant changing solid ingots into liquid. In fact, however, liquefaction consists of two phenomena:

- Heating a solid ingot to the melting point.
- Changing an ingot that has reached the melting point from a solid to a liquid by applying to it the latent heat of liquefaction.

Consequently, in one case, thermal efficiency increased 15 percent when excess heat generated by the furnace was used to raise temperatures to the critical point while the raw ingots or scrap were in the solid state.

A Bubble Is Composed of Two Elements

I used this example earlier to introduce the idea of looking at multiple goals. Now I'd like to return to it to make a related point.

To achieve uniformly dense coating material in an electrodeposition coating operation at T Industries, air was blown into the coating material and the mixture was agitated. As I mentioned earlier, this generated foam that spilled out of the vats and had to be disposed of.

The original solution had been to apply an antifoaming agent. This was effective, but it also proved to be both time-consuming and costly. Now a search was on for a cheaper, simpler way to remove the bubbles.

When I asked the young technician in charge what a bubble was, he merely blinked and made no reply.

"Perhaps there are bubbles getting in the way of your eyes," I teased him. Then I spoke more seriously: "A bubble," I said, "is composed of two things. The first is the air inside and the second is the film of coating material surrounding that air. Although right now you're trying to find some way to dissolve the film of coating material on the outside, how about giving some thought to removing the air on the inside?"

"So what do we do?" said Mr. H.

I immediately went to the shop floor and had him take a handful of foam. I slapped the foam with my hand and the bubbles vanished instantly. I thought about the effects of that sudden slap for a moment and then it struck me. I asked to have a washing machine brought and then filled the tub with foam. When we turned the machine on for a moment or so, the foam disappeared as quickly as the bubbles had earlier. Yet no liquid coating material drained out of the machine. When we had repeated this operation three times and still no liquid appeared, I suggested that we tilt the washing machine slightly. This allowed roughly a cupful of liquid coating material to drain out. Thus, three machine loads full of foam yielded only a cup of coating material. The remaining 99 percent of the foam was air.

Ultimately, the foam was broken down by forcing it through a fine screen with a stream of coating material.

The approach to the problem differed dramatically depending on whether we tried to break down the outer film of coating material or remove the air inside. It is important to recognize that errors can result when the fundamental conceptual approach is not correct.

There Are Three Methods of Heating

Mr. Horiuchi, an officially designated "intangible cultural treasure," is considered a master of "hand-rubbed teamaking." I once visited Mr. Horiuchi to observe his method of tea production. Once there, I noticed that, although charcoal had sufficed in the past for drying the tea, drying had been uneven ever since they had begun using propane gas. I happened to notice that results improved when an iron sheet was positioned between the propane gas and the tea rack.

"Why is the iron there?" I asked.

"We don't really know," was the reply, "but when we tried it things improved."

I thought about this for a moment and then turned to Mr. Horiuchi.

"Listen," I said, "heating can take place in three ways: by conduction, by convection, or by radiation. When you used charcoal, heat radiating from the glowing charcoal created convection currents on top and these dried the tea leaves as they passed through them.

"With propane gas, however, the strong flames heat the air in the center and this heat passes first through the middle of the tea racks. Yet this retards drying of the tea at the periphery, doesn't it, so the leaves do not dry uniformly?

"When a sheet of iron is placed in the middle, even when temperatures in the center are high, the iron conducts heat across its entire surface and radiation from the sheet in turn heats all the upper air by means of convection. This means that the tea is dried uniformly. In the final analysis, local heat from the propane gas burners is spread out across the entire surface by means of the iron sheet."

Here, the knowledge that things improved when an iron sheet was in place amounted to mere know-how. On the other hand, understanding why this improved things was "know-why": it is know-why that makes it possible to apply the same approach in many other situations.

Drying Is More than Mere Heating

It is widely believed that drying is synonymous with heating — that high temperature is the single important condition involved. In fact, however, other influential factors are at work.

Let us look at the process of drying magnetic rings used in sulfuric acid reactor columns in a chemical plant. Rings 50 mm thick by 60 mm were packed into a sheath and loaded onto a dolly. They were then exposed to hot air as they passed through a drying furnace in an operation that took four hours. The problem was to reduce drying time.

Here is what I suggested to Mr. Tatebayashi, the head of the Technology Division:

"Drying means causing moisture to evaporate and this involves three major influencing factors: temperature, humidity, and air speed. Your current method, placing rings in sheaths, relies principally on heat. With this method, though, evaporated moisture remains trapped inside the sheaths and ends up suppressing further evaporation. You could surely shorten drying times if you were to use moving air to blow this moisture away."

When a single ring placed on a grill was exposed to hot air in a dryer, it dried in only three minutes. Thus, with the old method of placing rings in sheaths, it was difficult for heat to reach the bottom and evaporated moisture remained trapped, hindering subsequent evaporation.

These shortcomings extended the drying time because drying was governed by the slowest drying items.

With the new method, however, each ring is dried separately. Heat reaches its entire surface, and evaporated moisture is blown away by moving air, which improves air replacement and speeds evaporation. The result is a significant reduction in drying time.

We ought to know that as long as there is a breeze, laundry on a clothesline will dry even on a cloudy day. This proves how important the effect of removing moisture can be.

In the introduction to this chapter I mentioned the drying of syrup used as the raw material for caramel at M Confectionary. Problems cropped up in the form of unexpectedly long melting times, thought to be the result of changes in syrup composition.

In fact, syrup cans were packed into drying ovens with almost no space between them, because increased production targets could not be met unless many cans were put in the oven at the same time.

"That won't work here," I said. "Separate the cans from one another."

"But we can't do that," was the response. "We won't keep up with production."

"Just try it," I urged.

I had them experiment with forcing hot air to circulate inside the ovens. As a result, even with a 60 percent reduction in the capacity of each load, it became possible to melt large quantities of syrup. What used to take two hours now took only 40 minutes. Significant effects were obtained by allowing heat to reach the entire surface of each item and by using new hot air to continuously remove any moisture generated.

Danger Interlocks and Safety Interlocks

Interlocking in automation means to assure safety by verifying the completion of one motion before moving on to the next motion. In a plastic molding operation, interlock functions were provided at each juncture between motions:

- A product removal device was activated and entered the mold after verifying that the mold had opened.
- After removing the product, the device retreated; motions to close the mold began when the removal device completed its motion.

These procedures were improved as follows:

1. Four-tenths of a second are saved by bringing the product removal device to within 50 mm of the mold while the mold is still closed.

2. Rather than starting the product removal device after the mold has completed its opening movement, the device is set in motion as soon as the two halves of the mold have moved apart by about 10 mm more than is necessary to permit entrance of the removal device. The point here is that since the mold is opening, the interlock is for motion in a safe direction. This cut 0.8 seconds off the previous time for the operation.

3. Next, rather than closing the molds after the product removal device had removed the product and completed its motion, 1.2 seconds were saved by beginning the closing motion as soon as the removal device had withdrawn to about 50 mm beyond the range of mold opening and closing movements. Here again, since the product removal device is moving away from the mold, the interlock involves motion in a safe direction.

Thus there are two types of interlocks: interlocks for movement toward danger — *danger interlocks* — and interlocks for movement toward safety — *safety interlocks*. If the product removal device is to enter the mold when the mold is closing, then a danger interlock is called for and safety must be verified before the device is set in motion. If the mold is in the process of opening, however, then the product removal device can be activated as soon as there is enough clearance so that the device will not interfere with the mold.

Thus, it helps to distinguish between danger and safety interlocks.

In this particular example, reducing times for safety interlocks cut a previous cycle time of 25 seconds to 22.6 seconds:

$$25 \text{ sec} - (0.4 \text{ sec} + 0.8 \text{ sec} + 1.2 \text{ sec}) = 22.6 \text{ sec.}$$

In terms of production output, this amounted to a real increase of 10.6 percent.

In another example involving a die casting machine, the following procedures were carried out:

- Clamp die halves.
- Using a toggle device, raise die clamping pressure to 500 tons.
- Pour in molten aluminum.

Here, the point of raising clamping pressure is to prevent molten aluminum from seeping out from joints between the halves of the die — this requires 500 tons of resistance. Yet, if molten aluminum is simply being poured in, there is no danger of its leaking even before such high pressure is applied. Consequently, by pouring in molten aluminum as soon as the die halves are clamped, interlock time can ordinarily be reduced by 1.4 seconds or so. If the cycle time is 35 seconds, this means a 4.2 percent increase in production:

$$35 \text{ sec} \div (35 \text{ sec} - 1.4 \text{ sec}) \times 100 = 104.2\%$$

Furthermore, as in the plastic molding case, taking another look at interlock times for product removal devices, as well as die separation agents, can usually cut times by about 3.5 seconds. This would amount to an additional two months' worth of production over the course of a year:

$$35 \text{ sec} \div (35 \text{ sec} - 3.5 \text{ sec} - 1.4 \text{ sec}) \times 100 = 116.3\%$$

Although it is generally assumed when installing automatic equipment that interlock mechanisms are provided to assure the safety of all motion, significant effects can sometimes be achieved unexpectedly by thinking about the problem in greater detail and by keeping in mind the distinction between danger interlocks and safety interlocks.

Z — SYSTEMATIC GOALS

Goals and Means Trade Places

We must learn to think of making progress as moving toward goals, because goals often become means at a higher level. When we think about a goal we are really considering the means toward an even higher-order goal. Thus, it is crucial to understand how goals and means "trade places."

For example, to achieve the goal of filling our bellies when we are hungry, we adopt the means of eating. Filling our bellies, however, is only a means for attaining the higher-order goal of taking in nourishment. Similarly, taking in nourishment is actually a means for attaining an even higher-order goal: maintaining life. Furthermore, the maintenance of life is perhaps nothing more than a means to the goal of species survival. At this point, the issue is largely controlled by one's view of life.

As we can see, goals and means trade places with one another in a chain, and the means or measures we choose will vary considerably depending upon what level of goal we recognize.

Similarly, the Toyota Production System's focus on the "5 Whys" emphasizes the fact that we can discover the true causes of things by asking why, why, why, why, and why over and over again. Unless we are aware that goals and means trade places with one another, and unless we persist in tracking each issue to its source, our improvements will remain superficial and inconclusive and we will never be able to improve in essential, fundamental ways.

"Know-how" Alone Isn't Enough! You Need "Know-why"!

Akira Shibata, executive director of Daihō Industries, once gave me a good piece of advice. Although it is considered important to have a firm grasp of "know-how", know-how is not enough by itself. He explained that "if know-how is all that's passed along, you may be able to perform a task the way it was taught, but you won't know what to do when conditions change or the least bit of trouble crops up. If, on the other hand, you also understand why things are the way they are — the 'know-why' of the task — then you will be able both to cope with changes, and to apply your knowledge to other tasks."

This impressed me as being right on the mark. All too often, people visit other plants only to copy their methods. Or, they are satisfied to learn know-how, but too lazy to raise know-how to know-why and find out *why* things are done the way they are. We must make the effort to grasp what lies behind even the most superficial method.

Ask the Drying Oven How Things Are Going

In drawing wire, the wire is dipped in lime water and then dried. This process took two hours at one plant; the people involved wanted to shorten this time.

I visited the plant and saw about a ton of coiled wire hanging on pipes and drying over oil burners. Not only did the wire take a long time to dry, but after the drying was complete, the hot wire needed roughly half an hour to cool down. Naturally, this created problems when expedited operations were required.

I asked the head of the wire-drawing department what he was doing in the operation.

"We're drying the drawn wire," he replied.

"Can't you do without drying the wire?"

"Not dry it?" he said. "No, no. It would be all sticky from the lime water and wouldn't be good for anything."

"Listen," I said. "What gets sticky isn't the wire at all. It's the lime water on the outside of the wire, isn't it?"

I immediately borrowed a portable dryer and managed, in a mere three minutes, to dry the lime water on the outside of the wire.

"How about it?" I said to the department head. "If we were to stand next to the drying oven and ask it how things were going, I bet we'd hear the wire inside calling out to say that it's too hot. 'All you have to do is dry the lime water on the outside of me!' it would shout."

This particular company official was a junior classmate of mine and he turned the tables on me:

"If we were to do silly things like that," he countered, "then we'd put you out of business."

He was right about that.

Does Heating Cause Distortion?

The myth that heating and cooling necessarily induce distortion is widely believed by plant technicians. Are they right? Absolutely not!

Heating does cause materials to expand, and cooling causes them to contract, but that does not necessarily mean heating or cooling will cause distortion. The problem is that the various parts of a product are not heated or cooled uniformly. Thus, the true cause of distortion is that temperatures are not raised or lowered uniformly or at a uniform speed.

At S Electric, in an operation for solenoid parts, two cylindrical parts were fit together. A ring of solder was placed between the two parts and then the parts were joined by melting the solder with a gas burner. In the method used, the product was held in a lathe chuck and the gas burner flame melted the solder and formed the joint as the product was slowly turned at a rate of about five revolutions per minute. Distortion seemed inevitable. The cylindrical joints became elongated and it took considerable effort to make them round again. There seemed to be no way to make the parts stay perfectly round.

When I suggested that the distortions should not be introduced in the first place, the plant manager maintained that heating inevitably generated distortions.

"Not at all," I replied. "What you have to do is to heat and cool the material uniformly."

This having been said, the following procedures were adopted for the operation:

- The rate of lathe rotation was increased to 300 revolutions per minute. With the burner flame blown against the workpiece, this high-speed rotation meant that the entire circumference was heated uniformly. The slow rotation used in the previous method had allowed only part of the circumference to be heated at a time which generated distortions.
- The burner flame — used to melt the solder — was reduced and then gradually enlarged. This allowed heat to be conducted adequately from the joint to the main body of the workpiece and therefore did away with abrupt temperature transitions near the joint.
- Similarly, when heating was completed, the burner flame was gradually reduced to avoid causing any extreme temperature changes.

These new procedures completely eliminated welding distortions and operations to correct distortion.

This experience dealt a mortal blow to the myth that heating necessarily induces distortion.

Polishing Welding Disks

At A Electric the bottoms of washing machine drainage tubs are seam-welded to the main bodies of the machines. When I suggested that the welding machine be run during the lunch hour since it did not need to go to the cafeteria for lunch, I immediately ran into opposition.

"We can't do that," I was told. "When the disk on the welder gets dirty it throws off sparks and causes welding defects. Not only that, but the defects are serial ones, so an operator has to be watching. If sparks begin to fly off, he can turn off the machine and regrind the disk to keep multiple defects from occurring.

"Since we don't know when sparks might appear, there always has to be an operator by the machine. There's no way we could run it unmanned during lunch hours."

"What causes the sparks?" I asked.

"The disk gets dirty from detergent at the joint, and sparks are generated when the detergent cuts off the electric current."

"Your problem," I said, "is that you're trying to polish the outside of the disk after the dirt has already accumulated. Why don't you polish the disk continuously so that it is always clean?"

"Can't do it," was the answer. "A welder disk is quite expensive and polishing it continuously would shorten its life and result in considerable loss."

"You can't know how much it will shorten the life of a disk unless you try it," I said. "Why not give it a shot?"

The following method was adopted:

- When each weld is completed and the disk withdraws from the welding surface, a buff polishes the disk's surface.

Results obtained were favorable:

- No sparks are ever generated because the disk surface is always clean, and because detergent never interrupts the electric current.
- Although there had been concern that disk life would be shortened, it has in fact been lengthened by about 30 percent. In the past, tiny pits dug out by sparks made it necessary to grind the disk by about 0.5 mm. Now, however, polishing involves less wear of the disks because all that must be ground away is accumulated dirt.

One obvious result of this improvement is that pre-automation can be carried out even during the lunch hour. This has increased productive capacity considerably. The shift from polishing disks after they became dirty to polishing them so they do not get dirty proved very effective.

Pole Plate Dipping

In manufacturing pole plates for storage batteries, a paste is applied to a hoop-shaped mesh sheet plate. After this has been dried, the large plate is sectioned into 300 mm × 200 mm pole plates, which are then dipped in a metallic solution.

The pole plates are hung up after dipping to remove droplets of liquid and then dried again. Inevitably, the coating was thicker toward the bottom. The thick portions were shaved away by brushing, but since this could not be done uniformly, product performance was unsatisfactory. The question then, was how to shave the excess off uniformly.

At the plant in question, the pole plates were hung parallel to the ground, dipped in the liquid and then hung up again. They were left there until they stopped dripping, then sent into a drying oven.

Seeing this, I asked my hosts, "Why do you suppose the coating gets thicker towards the bottom?"

"Well, it's because more metallic solution adheres to the bottom."

"Why don't you arrange for the coating to go on evenly?" I asked.

"That's what we want, but it's impossible."

"Why does it get thicker at the bottom?" I said. "When drops are big, they fall off, but as the volume of the drops decreases, surface tension causes them to accumulate at the bottom. This stops the flow of liquid at the top and the farther you go toward the bottom the more liquid adheres. Maybe you should think of some way to get rid of the drops that accumulate at the bottom."

"We thought of that, too," I was told, "and tried blowing jets of air at the bottom. It didn't work, though, because the liquid just slipped behind to the other side of the plates."

At this point, I made a suggestion:

- Hang the plates at a 45 degree angle rather than parallel to the ground.
- This will cause liquid to accumulate in the bottom corner, where the excess can be blown away with jets of air.

Implementing this approach eliminated the accumulation of drops that built up liquid at the bottom of each plate. The flow from the top was no longer obstructed, thus insuring that dipping alone would produce a uniform surface. The need to brush away excess coating was eliminated as well. The quantity of metallic solution used was also reduced. Since the solution was extremely expensive, this meant a monthly savings of ¥ 3 million ($15,000.)

Why Post Defect Statistics?

For the space of a month in April and May of 1985, I was invited as a consultant to visit ten U.S. firms, including major companies such as General Motors and McDonnell-Douglas. I was impressed by American enthusiasm for quality improvement, for everywhere I went, I saw posters proclaiming that "Quality is an American Tradition."

At Granville-Phillips, charts showing defect statistics were posted all around the plant. I asked the company president, Mr. Bills, why the charts were on display.

"It's so everyone will be concerned about defects and work to reduce them," he said.

"But these are like government mortality statistics that tell you how many people died of cancer and how many people died of strokes," I replied. "Posting them is no more than displaying post mortem certificates.

"What you ought to do is hunt down the defective elements in operations that generate a lot of defects. Unless you find and correct those elements, you're not likely to get very far. Could you let me take a look at the operation that is giving you the most trouble?"

I was taken to see a case-soldering operation near the end of the production process. In this process a printed circuit board and parts were mounted in the bottom of a center unit contained in a case approximately 150 mm in diameter. A ring of solder was placed around the circumference of the case and the case was rotated while a burner heated the solder.

Problems had arisen because excess heat from the burner was reaching the printed circuit board in the center unit. Even though the heat was separated from the boards by about 100 mm of tubing, roughly 10 percent of the assemblies still turned out to be defective.

After observing the operation for a while, I suggested to Mr. Bills that instead of aiming the burner flame directly at the center of the assembly, they aim the flame tangentially to the tube. We tried out this new method immediately, and out of ten units, not a single defect appeared.

The problem in this case was excess heat from the gas burner.

Rather than installing some sort of insulating device, it was better not to aim the heat in that direction in the first place. "In short," I said, "you have to provide sufficient heat to melt the solder, but where you aim the burner flame is a different problem entirely."

Six months later, a conference took me to Colorado. Mr. Bills had a cold at the time, but he sent me what I might describe as a "love letter": "In making this change we discovered that our header design has been defective for over seven years. A simple change here will give us 100 percent good parts." Thus, with no charts displayed, defects dropped dramatically, merely as a result of reevaluating operating procedures on the shop floor.

Mr. Bills's letter went on to say that they had succeeded in cutting welding setup times from 15 minutes to 1 minute. From that point on, everyone in the plant made it a habit to ask "why?" five times.

Mr. Bills and I have become great friends and I look forward with pleasure to our next meeting.

Measuring Isn't the Same as Verifying!

We use calipers and micrometers to measure things. But in doing so, is our real purpose to measure or to verify? If, for example, we take a measurement in order to know how much material needs to be cut away, then we are undoubtedly measuring to obtain a measure. Yet, when we measure items to find out whether they are satisfactory or not, we are measuring in order to verify conformance to standard. In these cases we can get by using gauges.

Even though we may use measurement as a way to perform inspection, examining the purposes of such procedures reveals that around 95 percent of the measurement is carried out to ascertain conformance to standards. Measuring to obtain a measure amounts to no more than 5 percent.

In brief, we need to recognize clearly what our true goals are and avoid confusing means with ends.

Change Adjustments to Settings

At U Television, adjustment was the final stage of the television assembly process. Skilled workers looked at waves on an oscilloscope and tightened an adjustment screw accordingly. The process took a long time and demanded a high level of skill. After watching the task for a while, I turned to the head of the Manufacturing Division and asked him whether the actual purpose of the task was to adjust the television sets. "It seems to me," I said, "that the real job is to find the right settings."

"What do you mean?"

"When I watch the task as it's being performed now, the worker turns the adjustment screw first to the right and then to the left. This is clearly adjusting. Even so, the real task is surely to set the screw at the proper place."

"If that's true, then all the worker should have to do is turn the screw to the left or right and stop at the proper place."

We then made the following changes:

- Oscilloscope waveforms were converted into numerical voltage readings.
- Because it was difficult to make small turns of 3 mm adjustment screws with a small screwdriver, a 60 mm diameter circular plate was mounted on the driver. With a graduated scale at the circumference of this plate, screws could be turned by as little as one-twentieth of a revolution, making it possible to stop turning precisely when the numerical readout reached zero.

These improvements permitted ordinary workers to perform the task and cut the time required for the job in half. In the final analysis, improving the precision of settings enabled the plant to eliminate adjustments.

Removing Paint from Masks Does Not Necessarily Mean Dissolving the Paint

Painting often involves the use of masks to ensure that only certain areas are painted. Paint adheres to the masks, however, and removing the paint often turns into a major problem. Typically, the mask is soaked in thinner to dissolve paint adhering to the surface. Since this is not done until after the mask has been used many times, removing the paint from the mask takes quite a long time.

Yet removing paint from a mask does not necessarily mean dissolving the paint. It simply means taking paint off the surface of the mask. Thus, it is more effective to strip paint off with a blade or a brush. The entire procedure can be completed in a very short time if only the remaining paint is dissolved with thinner.

In any event, it is crucial to recognize that the goal is to *remove* paint, not *dissolve* it.

Furthermore, while it may be effective to dissolve paint with thinner where the paint buildup is slight, other successful techniques include agitating the mask, spraying on thinner, or soaking the mask in a moving stream of thinner.

Use Washing to Prevent Buildups Rather than to Remove Buildups

Machine tools generate cuttings and sometimes these cuttings are removed by a worker with a brush. Because this is inefficient, oil or some other fluid can be used to wash away shavings. Cuttings are not always easily washed away, however. The job is much simpler if cuttings are washed away continuously rather than after large clumps have accumulated. An important trick, then, is to use washing to prevent buildups rather than to remove buildups.

Too Much Play in the Machine

In production plants everywhere you will hear complaints that poor product precision is caused by too much play in the machines. But is that really true?

At Z Industries, a machine called a double sizer cut the two sides of sinks to specified dimensions. The width did not always come out precisely, however, and recurring errors of 0.5 mm–1.0 mm meant that manual adjustments had to be made later. The shop's explanation for this was too much play in the machine.

"You say there's too much play in the machine," I commented, "and you certainly have a problem if that play causes clamping bolts to loosen after the saw has been set in the proper position.

But even with play in the feed bolts for determining width, you should be able to get by with 350 mm ± 0.

The problem isn't that the feed bolts allow too much play — it's the degree of precision to which you should set the width. Play in the machine would have an effect if you're feeding back to front, but if you're bringing the units in from the side, play shouldn't have any effect at all."

I had them buy a magnascale with numerical readout so that dimensions could be set more precisely. This brought variations in product width into the 5/1,000 mm range and made it possible to obtain the correct width merely by cutting. There was no longer any need for later adjustments.

In most cases when the blame for unsatisfactory precision is attributed to play in the machine, the real cause lies in imprecise measurements.

There Are Two Distinct Types of Welding Distortion

In any production plant, welding generates distortions that can be quite difficult to remove. It is widely thought, in fact, that these distortions are inevitable — people often just give up trying to do anything about them.

There are, however, two distinct types of welding distortion:

1. *External distortions*: where distortions cause changes in shape
2. *Internal distortions*: where shape does not change, but internal structure is altered; in extreme cases cracks appear

External distortions generally give the most trouble. To weld something, we normally place it on a workbench or — if we secure it — we typically use some simple means of holding pieces down so they do not slip wildly apart. External distortion can be prevented, however, if before welding we join the pieces as closely as possible with a force that can withstand the powerful forces involved in welding.

This will induce internal distortion, however, and do violence to the structure of the material. To avoid this, the welded section can be heated with a burner for a few minutes after welding to anneal it. At the same time, internal structure can be stabilized by letting the weld cool naturally and slowly.

Using this procedure, external distortions occur rarely and can be limited to extremely minor deformations. Operations to remove distortions can be dispensed with as well.

6

Basic Approaches to Improvement

III. Better Means

No improvement could take place in this world if there were only a single means to each end. Indeed, it is only when one believes in the existence of multiple means that the possibility of improvement first appears.

Progress will never pay a visit to those who stubbornly insist that their way is right and no other means are possible. Yet if we keep an open mind and believe that there are several possible means to each end, improvement ideas will emerge through the process of selecting the best method.

Thus, the single most important prerequisite for improvement is an open mind.

MULTIPLE MEANS TO A SINGLE END

If we believed there were only one means to each end, any sort of improvement would be impossible.

Yet, all too often we imagine that only our current methods will bring about the ends we are aiming for. Even if we don't make that assumption, we frequently persuade ourselves that current methods are the best. These attitudes will ensure that improvement never takes place. Indeed, we may even end up believing that current methods are goals in themselves.

Our current approach is never more than a means. Beyond it lies another goal, which is itself only a means toward a higher goal. If we understand this and pursue our goal vigorously, we can expect to discover even better methods. At the same time, even more means will present themselves if we consider our goals or ends from a variety of perspectives.

If today is going to be any different from yesterday, we must blaze new trails every day.

Smoothing Rough Surfaces with Unhulled Rice

At one company, sandpaper was used to smooth the rough surfaces inevitably remaining on pressure-formed ebonite switch holders. Ebonite is hard and brittle, so that whereas rubbing it too hard could damage the material, rubbing it lightly took a great deal of time. The task was made all the more frustrating because the sandpaper wore out quickly.

At this point a decision was made to place the product in a drum with an abrasive and rotate the drum to remove the rough surfaces. No suitable abrasive could be found, however. Steel pellets were tried first, but they produced defects in the form of rounded edges. Plastic beads were tried next, but this time the abrasive material wore down too quickly. Moreover, efficiency was poor because it took such a long time to smooth the rough surfaces. A variety of tests were conducted to find an abrasive that could satisfy the contradictory demands of softness and sharp cutting ability, but no suitable substance turned up.

Eventually, Mr. A, the second son of a farmer, recalled that his family used to remove the dirty skins of potatoes by rotating them in unhulled rice. When he suggested using unhulled rice in the plant, everyone laughed at the idea and said it was silly, but the plant manager was willing to give the idea a try.

Excellent results were obtained from a test using the rice. The folds in each rice grain are knife-sharp, but the air inside the grain makes it soft overall. The rice did not damage the product or take a long time to smooth the rough surfaces.

Too often we reject ideas we have tested only in our heads. Even approaches that seem ridiculous, however, cannot be evaluated unless we give them a try. I have had numerous experiences in which — despite advice to the contrary — actually testing an idea yielded first-rate results. If someone suggested to you that unhulled rice would make an excellent abrasive for smoothing rough surfaces, would you immediately agree to give the idea a try? When we have the courage to try them, such unexpected methods often lead to success.

Attaching Fiberglass

This example involves the construction of boats used to collect edible seaweed in the Ariake Sea off the island of Kyūshū.

The outer hull of each boat was made of a plastic material, and several layers of fiberglass attached with adhesives to the interior made the boats both strong and light. The boats were popular because they lasted a long time; unlike wooden boats they were not subject to rotting.

Y Industries had learned how to manufacture these boats from a high-tech plant in Osaka, but it could not manage to produce a high-quality product. Labor costs were unexpectedly high, and the business was not profitable. For these reasons, I was called in to observe the operation.

- First, fiberglass was attached and then painted with adhesive.
- This inevitably trapped air inside, so holes were bored to remove air bubbles.
- The surface was rubbed with a roller to distribute the remaining air bubbles uniformly.

When these air removal and air bubble dispersion operations were not carried out carefully, the hulls could break. These operations became the crucial factors determining quality.

The plant manager hoped there might be some quick, easy method for removing air and dispersing bubbles by machine rather than by hand. He lamented that things were not going smoothly even though his plant adhered faithfully to the know-how it had learned from the plant in Osaka.

After observing the operation for a while, I suggested to the plant manager that a better method existed.

"A better method?" he exclaimed, "what method is that?"

"All you have to do," I said, "is to attach the fiberglass so that air can't get into it in the first place."

"That won't work. Air gets in even at the plant in Osaka."

"What you must do is simply dip the fiberglass into the adhesive," I said.

In the new procedure, then, the adhesive is kept in a container, and sheets of fiberglass are dipped into the liquid adhesive. Since the liquid adhesive seeps into the fiberglass from below, any air inside the fiberglass is pushed out the top. This method completely eliminates air bubbles in the glass wool.

Now the whole operation is conducted as follows:

- Adhesive is first spread generously on the inside of the hull.
- Fiberglass is spread on top.
- When the adhesive has soaked through and risen to the top, a roller is applied to the entire surface and all air is removed.
- Another generous layer of adhesive is applied on top.
- Fiberglass is spread on top.

Thus, the operation has essentially been reversed. Before, adhesive was spread over the fiberglass; now, the fiberglass over a coating of adhesive. This improvement resulted in extremely high quality and reduced labor costs to one-fifth of what they were.

In the final analysis, it would have been better if more rigorous thought had been given to the essential nature of the task.

Coating Washers with Rustproofing Oil

In this operation the surfaces of spring washers are coated with rustproofing oil. Originally, this was carried out as follows:

- Place a number of washers in a cage and dip into liquid rustproofing oil.
- Place cage in a holding area to allow excess oil to drain off.
- After washers have dried to a certain degree, collect washers, count out specified number, and place in packing crates.

Even though workers carried out this task wearing rubber gloves, the rustproofing oil inevitably harmed their hands. There were complaints from the shop floor, furthermore, that it was difficult to carry out the operation with gloves on. This was a job no one enjoyed — especially because the workers were female part-timers who very much disliked the fact that it was rough on their hands.

I suggested the following improvements:

- Specified numbers of dried spring washers are placed in packing crates.
- Rustproofing oil is sprayed onto the tops of the washers.

The group leader opposed this idea, saying that the oil would not coat the entire surfaces of washers that were close together. We made a trial run anyway and obtained magnificent results. Although only the tops of the washers were sprayed, the rustproofing oil spread to the entire surface of each washer through osmosis. An appropriate amount of oil adhered to each washer, so that quality actually improved. Unlike before, there was no excess. No oil at all adhered to workers' hands and complaints of rough hands ended. Moreover, the amount of rustproofing oil used, dropped to one-tenth of what it had been.

We should never assume that an idea for improvement will not work. Only by giving it a try can we know for certain whether it will work.

Peeling the Protective Film Off Double-Stick Tape

Quite a few jobs these days involve sticking double-sided adhesive material to the backs of nameplates or labels and then attaching these items to fenders or other parts. To prevent these adhesives from sticking to other items during handling, the adhesive surfaces are protected by thin vinyl films. Peeling off this protective film, however, can be a considerable chore.

In many cases, a worker inserts a fingernail between the adhesive and the film and then peels off the entire film. Workers dislike this operation, though, because after peeling off a number of films, fingernails break and fingertips show signs of wear and tear.

At Y Synthetics, workers were unhappy about this peeling operation and would not do it for long. At this point the following suggestion was made: "Why not use a nozzle to blow compressed air under the corner of the protective film? Since very different effects will be obtained depending on the angle of the nozzle, test a number of angles to find the best one."

Tests were begun immediately. They showed that this technique not only lifted the corner of the film — it blew the entire film off. At this point, a special mechanism was constructed:

- The compressed air nozzle was secured at a suitable angle.
- The nozzle was flattened and squared off so that it emitted a knife-shaped jet of air.
- When a nameplate is pressed into a certain position, the compressed air is blown out.

- The protective film that has been peeled off is held by a vacuum suction device and placed in a trash bin.
- Although the 4 kg/mm^2 air pressure ordinarily used in the plant was sufficient to do the job, using 6 kg/mm^2 in cases of powerful adhesion nearly always allowed the protective film to come off by itself.

This completely eliminated complaints about painful fingernails.

Stripping Apart Sheet Metal

Occasionally during processing, materials stick together and pieces enter machines on top of one another. Although it is often believed that pieces adhere to one another because of grease, this is simply wrong. The correct way to understand the real cause is to see it as the effect, not of adhesion, but of vacuum suction. At the same time, however, the presence of grease, under the weight of a sheet of metal, can have a sealing effect.

It follows then, that to prevent materials from sticking to one another, all that is needed is to eliminate the vacuum between sheets of metal. Some strategies for achieving this are described below.

Blow pressurized air between the sheets.

1. The 4 kg/mm^2 air supplied in production plants is usually sufficient, but at one company, 4 kg/mm^2 did not work. However, 6 kg/mm^2 cleanly separated the pieces.
2. It is crucial that the stream of air be directed toward the juncture between the sheets. Consequently, a mechanism must be devised that pushes up the material and keeps the surface sheet in a fixed location. Furthermore, the angle of the stream of the air is significant and can be determined through trial and error.
3. Since the vacuum between two sheets is destroyed by driving a wedge of air into the space between them, it is more effective to use a thin, squared-off nozzle than a normal round one.

Draw the pieces apart with a saw blade. Sheets can be stripped apart by drawing a rough metal saw backwards at a 45° – 60° angle across the edges of the sheets to form a gap and then by introducing air into the gap. In manual operations, it is convenient to mount a saw blade on a ring and wear it facing out on the middle finger, so that it does not get in the way of other operations.

The bending method. Doubled sheets can be peeled apart by attaching a long rod fitted with suction cups to the middle of the sheet and bending the sheets as you lift them. This technique is also effective when used along with compressed air.

Occasionally, magnets are used at the ends of the rod, but this is unsuitable because magnetism will draw the sheets together. Vacuum suction is a more effective method because it draws up only one of the sheets.

The bump method. Even when two sheets are in close contact, the formation of a vacuum can be prevented by making three or four suitably spaced 1 mm bumps on sections that will be trimmed off and discarded later. This method provides the surest way to prevent sheets from adhering to one another.

The phased-roll method. Although this method cannot necessarily be applied to sheet metal, it was useful in a case where paper for making ice cream cups tended to double up.

In this particular instance, a phased-roll method was used:

1. 40 mm diameter rolls were set up in pairs.
2. With the upper roll rotating clockwise and the bottom roll rotating counterclockwise, the paper was fed through from right to left.
3. The rolls were phased so that the top roll turned ten times for each five rotations of the bottom roll.
4. When a double layer of paper was fed through, the paper on top went through first, neatly peeling the pieces of paper from one another. The effect is the same as if one were to hold the paper between both hands and slide off the top sheet.

Double thickness sensors. Sensors can be used to detect double thicknesses, which are then sent to a bypass or separated manually.

The Purpose of Business Cards Is to Help People Remember Your Name

One day I went to say hello to the newly appointed foreman at our woodworking plant. I held out my business card and spoke a few formulaic words of greeting: "My name is Shingo. I'm in charge of planning. I expect I will be indebted to you in the future and hope that I may count on your kind consideration."

The foreman took my card, examined it for a moment, and then replied, "Oh, so you're in charge of planning?"

Then he slowly reached into his pocket and pulled out a wooden plaque and held it out for me to see.

"This is me," he said.

On the plaque was written:

> *Teiji Ikawa, Woodworking Shop Foreman*
> *Iwate Prefecture 1927*
> *Tōhoku University, Machine Science*

I looked at it, speechless.

"All right?" the foreman asked. When I nodded, he returned the plaque to his pocket.

I was astonished by the originality of the foreman's card, and on the way back to my office, I concluded with admiration that since the purpose of a business card is to get other people to remember your name, Mr. Ikawa had the right idea.

Rubber Stretches

This example involves the job of wrapping rubber edging around the ends of mattresses.

The main bodies of the mattresses were also made of rubber, so they would slip during cutting. Since precise circumferential dimensions for the mattresses could not be obtained, the edging material was cut a little longer than necessary, and any excess remaining after wrapping was cut off with shears and discarded. Cutting off the excess with shears impeded efficiency and wasted the edging. The people in charge of the operation wondered if there were some way to improve the procedure so that shears would not have to be used.

The prevailing opinion on the shop floor was that standardizing the dimensions of the edging was impossible since the mattresses were also made of rubber and variations in mattress size occurred during cutting.

Even so, we measured the circumferences of ten mattresses, found a mean value, and cut edging to that length. After the edging was secured to three sides of a mattress, it was stretched a bit if it turned out to be too short to fit around the remaining side. If it was too long, the ends were glued in place and several small tucks were taken in the middle to make it fit more snugly. This eventually made it possible to attach edging of a constant length and eliminated both excess scrap and the need for shears.

The head of the company's manufacturing section made a lasting impression on me when he recalled this episode afterwards. "Of course!" he said. "Stretching and contracting is what rubber does!"

In the final analysis, it was more productive to think of rubber's elasticity as an advantage than as a drawback.

Small Minds Want More Space

"The plant is too small."

"This operation needs more room."

Such complaints are heard quite often in production plants. When you look a little further into the matter, however, these pleas for more space are frequently the products of small minds. For example, take the complaint that "the plant is too small." Again and again, when we actually examine the plant in question, we find that the space occupied by idle work-in-process takes up 70 percent of the total area. As often as not, this idle space can be reduced by diminishing processing lot sizes, and it can be obviated entirely by instituting one-piece flow operations in earlier and subsequent processes.

As for the lament that "this operation needs more room," space requirements can be dramatically cut by increasing the frequency of parts supply or by setting up parts storage areas in three dimensions so as to cut down on the floor space such storage occupies.

Surprisingly, the opportunity to use space above and below conveyors is often missed. Rotating parts bins also make it possible to cut back tremendously on the "domain of operations."

To summarize:

- Use vertical space.
- Since available room is determined by the interaction of space and time, cutting idle time in half means to cut room needed for storage in half.

In any case, it is essential to realize that it is a small mind that wants more space.

Not Enough Resourcefulness

Sometimes when I go into a production plant and try to do something new, I am told that it will not work because "there aren't enough people" or "there aren't enough machines." Quite often, though, the real problem is not enough resourcefulness. Often when we look closely at the problem and observe the work area, possibilities for creating extra workers present themselves because, for example:

- No more than 30 percent of the people are doing useful work.
- Simple devices will allow some procedures to be mechanized.
- Machine operators can run other machines while their own machines are engaged in automatic processing.

Moreover, when we take the time to really look at the operation of machines, we find a surprising number of instances in which main processing operation times are short and much of the work is taken up by auxiliary operations, such as mounting and removing items.

In one example, holes in the bottoms and the handles of electric rice cookers were drilled in two separate processes. When I suggested that these be combined in one process, I was told that the machine lacked the capacity to drill all the holes at the same time.

"You claim that the machine doesn't have the capacity to drill all the holes at the same time," I said, "so why not just use what volleyball players call 'delayed spiking?' Drill the side holes an instant after drilling the bottom hole."

The suggestion worked beautifully and production increased twofold.

In this case, the idea of conducting a single process suggested mounting and removal from the machine at the same time. In contrast, I realized that saying that the machine had insufficient capacity implied that it could not function with both loads simultaneously. All that was needed, however, was to give the machine a time lag. There are many cases in a plant where problems can be solved in a similar way — by using your head and your resourcefulness.

"Because" Never Solves Anything

The "National Because League" is one of the most powerful groups in Japan. How often we say, "It won't work because of this" or "It's impossible because of that." The arguments we come up with are cogent and plentiful.

But no matter how many persuasive reasons we cite, no problem was ever solved by arguing in terms of "because."

The biggest problems, however, are the words that come after the "because." The final answer to the problem will depend on whether we say, "It won't work because of this, so let's give up" or "It won't work because of this, but how could we do it so that it will work?"

Since we are discussing real problems, it is inevitable that the first thing we think of when a problem is raised is *why* something will not work. Whether many plans for improvement will see the light of day, however, depends on the next thing we think. Will we say, "It won't work because of such and such" or "How can we make it work?"

This is the difference between "assuming" and "thinking."

Is the Weather Bad on Rainy Days?

We say that the weather is bad on rainy days. But is this in fact true?

Think about what would happen if it did not rain at all over the course of a year. It would be disastrous — crops would not grow and there would be no water to drink.

We make an extremely self-serving value judgment when we say rainy days are bad simply because they are not convenient for our plans.

Maybe we should ask what other major errors we commit in using ordinary expressions without thinking.

Mean Values Are Maximally Undependable Values

The concept of mean values is often considered important in our understanding of phenomena. In fact, however, a mean value is nothing more than the average of actual values and is not in any way an expression of fact.

Although mean values may be convenient for grasping overall tendencies, maximum values or minimum values are frequently more significant when we actually want to improve a task. Asking what generates the differential between maximum values and minimum values often gives us information that can help us identify areas needing improvement.

In brief, as we try to understand phenomena, we must decide whether we want merely to perceive the outline of a problem, or whether we want to comprehend it so that we can find a solution and make improvements.

7

Stage Three: Making Plans for Improvement

This chapter outlines the steps involved in actually putting together plans for improvement.

LOCKING IN ON THE PROBLEM

We lock in on a problem when we're not satisfied with the way a job is performed and ask why a particular method is used. At this stage there is doubt and dissatisfaction with the status quo — doubt and dissatisfaction that arose in response to a thorough pursuit of goals, when we asked, "What are the real objectives of this job?" As we saw in Chapter Five, the problem should be considered from all angles:

- X: focus
- Y: identify multiple goals
- Z: systematically pursue higher-order goals

At this stage, no thought whatsoever should be given to specific ideas. If an idea comes up, we may make a note of it, but we must not be imprisoned by it. This weakens the spirit of criticism and hinders locking in on subsequent problems. In this sense, it is extremely important that *locking in on the problem* be separated from *brainstorming*.

Keep Locking In on Problems Separate from Brainstorming

Locking in on a problem occurs when we entertain doubts about the status quo and formulate specific criticisms. Brainstorming, on the other hand, is our response to having locked in on a problem; essentially it involves coming to terms with reality. In this sense, just as there are positive and negative mental activities, the functioning of the mind is said to involve the interplay of both locking in and brainstorming.

It follows that brainstorming immediately after locking in on a problem will neutralize and weaken the critical mind and, in the end, few plans for improvement will be forthcoming. Thus, it is crucial to keep the process of locking in on a problem separate. In other words, we concentrate on that task alone and avoid thinking of specific ideas for change. If an idea comes up, we may make a note of it *and then forget it*. A desirable approach is to begin thinking of ideas that correspond to various observations we've made only *after* the last observation about the status quo has been made.

The observations that we make in locking in on problems *do not* foreshadow specific ideas; they are purely an intensive search for goals, the focusing of our attention — through exhaustive criticism — on why certain things are done. It is perfectly acceptable if:

- Two ideas are forthcoming for observation 1.
- There are no ideas for observation 2.
- No ideas at all come to mind for observation 3.
- There are five ideas for observation 4.

Someone else may come along and say "Hey! I've got an idea for that." Or we may hit on more ideas later on.

In any event, observing or locking in on problems is the key that opens a rich treasure house of improvement ideas, and this is why it is important to record observed problems separately even if no ideas for dealing with them immediately present themselves. The treasure house may look empty in the morning, but the afternoon sunshine can illuminate new discoveries. How we look at things changes over time and new ideas for dealing with problems show up suddenly where none were visible before.

The act of locking in on problems sows the seeds for improvement; strict separation of observing and brainstorming is an invariable condition for generating many improvements.

BRAINSTORMING

During the brainstorming stage, we come up with the means of responding to goals.

Since a single goal or end can have a number of means associated with it, numerous ideas can undoubtedly address a single observed problem. Moreover, if there are what we may term parallel ideas for approaching a given problem — for example, securing objects with bolts or with cams — there are also completely different alternatives conceivable (such as securing objects via interlocking).

Just as there are highly suitable ideas, there will also be ideas to be discarded. It does not matter, in short, if ideas overlap or contradict one another; every effort should be made to come up with large numbers of them. Group brainstorming can be extremely effective for this.

At this stage, judgment is inappropriate. Making judgments about tentative ideas will end up nipping them in the bud. In other words, brainstorming must focus solely on generating ideas without any type of criticism.

Keep Brainstorming Separate from Judgment

Brainstorming, in which various ideas for improvement are proposed, is a creative process, while judgment, in which specific aspects of ideas are rejected, is a critical process. Quite often, we may withhold ideas if we were worried that someone might criticize them. Since this is undesirable, it is important, in formulating plans for improvement, to have any and all ideas put forward at the brainstorming stage without any criticism whatsoever, and to have judgment begin only *after* all ideas have been presented.

Not only is criticism (judgment) by others inadvisable, it is undesirable for an individual to criticize his or her own ideas immediately after having aired them. When someone is coming up with ideas, it is important for him or her to bear in mind that *judgment comes later*. This is an absolute precondition for generating improvement plans in large numbers. According to a psychologist's report, over 60 percent more ideas are generated in an atmosphere where there is no criticism whatsoever.

We have already said that locking in on problems should be kept separate from brainstorming, but it is 100 times more vital to keep brainstorming absolutely separate from judgment. This, indeed, is the essence of brainstorming.

Shin-Tō Plastics set up what it calls a brainstorming room and displayed on its walls both set procedures for coming up with ideas and the Four Rules of Brainstorming. "No criticism may take place in this room," it is stipulated. "A fine of ¥100 will be levied for each criticism." This has reportedly put an end to the custom of criticism.

Resourcefulness and Money Offset One Another

How often we hear that someone would like to make improvements but is hampered by the cost! Actually, since resourcefulness and money offset one another, someone with little resourcefulness must use a great deal of money, while someone with a great deal of resourcefulness can get by with very little money. The superior improvement scheme uses little money and a great deal of resourcefulness.

We need to realize that complaints about inadequate this or that really boil down to inadequate resourcefulness. This brings to mind the following story.

H Industries manufactures metal parts for automobiles, and numerous magnetic conveyors are used on its processing lines. These conveyors grip pieces of metal and transport them vertically by running conveyors along magnetic surfaces. The devices provide quite a convenient means of transportation because metal pieces of any size or shape can be moved securely either up or down.

One day, the purchasing manager for a customer came to visit the plant. After seeing a conveyor, he took off a piece of metal that was being transported and brought it near some iron filings. When he did, the residual magnetism in the metal picked up all the filings. "We can't have residual magnetism in the metal," he said. "I want you to get rid of all your magnetic conveyors."

The plant used so many magnetic conveyors that getting rid of them would have posed a considerable problem, so at this point I was consulted about what might be done. I immediately went to the plant and observed the situation there. Then I addressed myself to the head of the production department:

"There's no reason to get rid of your magnetic conveyors," I said. "Since all you have to do is keep residual magnetism out of metal pieces delivered to D Technical Research Industries, why not look into a demagnetizer?"

When I visited the same plant the following month, I asked what had happened about the demagnetizer.

"Demagnetizers are available," I was told, "but they run as much as ¥1.5 million ($5,000) — so expensive that we've held back on using them." In response to this, I made another suggestion to the production department head: "Why don't you study a demagnetizer and find out exactly what the central mechanism is that actually demagnetizes?"

A month later I went to the plant again and the department head reported that they had made a demagnetizer. Right away, I went to the shop floor where metal pieces were being completely demagnetized as they passed beneath two simple magnetos mounted above the conveyor line at the final inspection process.

In the final analysis, the commercial demagnetizers turned out to be expensive because of various accessory devices, and the real demagnetization function merely involved passing objects through the magnetos' magnetic field. Thus, an investment of around ¥100,000 ($300) made it possible to demagnetize the metal pieces, and this eliminated subsequent claims from the customer.

Often, improvement can be had at a surprisingly modest price by thoroughly hunting down the real issues involved. Indeed, perhaps this is an example of improvement through resourcefulness rather than money.

If You Can't Push, Pull!

M Refining is a company whose business includes refining copper. The refining involved shooting fuel into a furnace through stainless steel pipes, but since the ends of the pipes melt, it was necessary to push them gradually into the furnace. Because the end of the pipe would be deformed and encrusted with slag at the end of the refining operation, the walls of the furnace would sometimes rupture under the considerable force required to withdraw the remaining pipe. This reduced furnace efficiency, because the next refining procedure could not begin until after the hour or so it took to repair the furnace walls and dry the fire-resistant clay.

This situation has been improved so that the furnace is now out of commission for a mere five minutes. The procedure is as follows:

1. A joint is used to couple the stainless steel pipe to a soft steel pipe.
2. The pipe is pushed bit by bit into the furnace as refining proceeds.
3. After the molten material has been expelled at the end of the refining process, the soft steel pipe is uncoupled at the joint and several blows of a hammer are used to propel the shortened stainless steel pipe into the furnace.

This prevents any deformed section of pipe from protruding from the furnace; it both removes the danger of rupturing furnace walls and obviates the use of considerable force.

The marvelous lesson in improvement to be drawn from this is that while past thinking had concentrated exclusively on *pulling* the pipe out, all that was really needed was to remove the pipe from where it had lodged. Pulling it out was one method of accomplishing this, but *pushing* it into the furnace was an equally valid approach.

In another operation, automobile seats were inserted with bands into which hot wires were woven. The problem was that wrinkles formed when a ruler was used to *push* the bands inside. These wrinkles were easily eliminated and the operation performed much more rapidly when a ruler inserted from the opposite side was used to catch the bands and *pull* them through.

Here again, it is aptly said, "If you can't push, pull!" or "If you can't pull, push!"

Checking at Specific Times and Checking Specific Items

Surveys are often carried out at specific time intervals to build a comprehensive picture of the status of work-in-process. For example, work-in-progress items may be checked daily, every ten days, or monthly. Often, however, carrying out these surveys can be quite tedious.

At the M Plant, checking work-in-process at the end of each day consumed a great deal of time and energy. I suggested the following procedure:

- Have a display register every 100 products.
- Supply parts needed for the product in groups of 100.

This checks whether the number of products matches the number of parts. We then arranged it so that the end-of-the-day check covered only items not accounted for in the continuous checks, with the result that it became possible to gain a simple and accurate picture of work-in-process.

Furthermore, when we supplied the number of products corresponding to a week's worth of replacements for defective items, we were able to replace defects when they occurred and end up with constant totals. This prevented defects from generating numerical discrepancies.

This approach of measuring specific quantities of items rather than checking at specific time intervals is by far the more effective.

Join Forces to Root Out Empty Motions

A Mr. Morita of T Industries once attended one of my production technology seminars. When he returned to the company, he reported to the managing director, Mr. N, that the seminar had been an exceptionally good one. "That stuff is all empty theorizing," was Mr. N's response. "I want to see some concrete evidence you've learned something useful." The director then had Mr. Morita transferred from a machine plant to an auto body plant to take charge of a new production group. After several months of working on improvements, Mr. Morita began to show marked success and the director reportedly changed his mind about him.

After this episode, I asked Mr. Morita what improvements he had instituted. "I tried," he explained, "to eliminate point 9 of motion analysis — that is, shifting back and forth or repositioning." In other words, he got rid of useless motions and improved operations by:

- Changing the placement of parts.
- Orienting items automatically.
- Providing guides to make insertion easier.

According to workers on the shop floor, Mr. Morita's improvements "somehow made the job easier." Empty motions had made jobs difficult and shop workers had to lend their efforts to rooting them out. Other calls for improvement followed from the shop and in the end Mr. Morita was able to achieve substantial results.

Curves Can Come In Handy

"Nearly all of the items we make are curved on one side," I was once told. There were various reasons for this:

- To ease the "bite".
- To serve as a guide to make fitting easier.
- To give a "soft" feel to the shape.

This example comes from Morinaga Confectionery, where there was an operation to align biscuits uniformly. It used to be that three workers would turn over any biscuits that were upside down. This procedure was improved, however, as follows (see Figure 6):

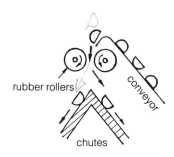

FIGURE 6. Biscuit Alignment Operation

- Products are lined up one by one and move upward on a conveyor. Some of them are facing up and some of them are facing down.
- When the products pass through a pair of rubber rollers — 50 mm in diameter — mounted at the top of the conveyor,

the top of the curved section of each biscuit facing down strikes the roller on the left, shifts to the right, and slides down the chute.

- The top of the curved section of each biscuit facing up strikes the right-hand roller, shifts to the left, and slides down the chute.

This simple device automatically distinguishes between items facing up and items facing down. In the same way, it is extremely handy to use curves when you want to sort objects automatically. In fitting items into one another, too, a curved surface on the part to be inserted can make the motion much easier.

Indiscriminate Air and Appropriate Air

Pressurized air is widely used in production plants. Close observation of the situations in which it is used, however, reveals the following points:

- Air is used where it is not really needed.
- Air is used where other easy methods are available.
- In situations where air is actually used, most of it is wasted in terms of the objectives desired.

This is what we might term *indiscriminate air.*

In contrast, there are situations that involve *appropriate air*: instances in which the use of air is ideal and effective. Although we tend to make the simplistic assumption that pressurized air is right for myriad tasks, it is important to give careful consideration to the fact that there are two types of air: indiscriminate air and appropriate air.

Build a Panama Canal in the Plant

The Panama Canal in Central America crosses a high isthmus to allow ships to pass from the Pacific Ocean to the Atlantic Ocean. A ship begins by proceeding to the first lock. The gates close and water pours in. When the water has risen to the level of water in the second lock, gates open and the ship proceeds to the second zone. The same process is repeated until the ship has reached the highest point. Then the reverse procedure begins and the ship descends to the Atlantic Ocean.

The same sort of idea can be applied in the production plant. For example, where long rods slide sideways down a chute, oddly shaped or bent rods or those with uneven friction resistance will often tilt and fall off. When such rods slide sideways down a chute, there is a safety margin within which little tilting occurs. This zone will vary according to the nature of the rods, but generally it is on the order of 300 mm. Installing stoppers in the chute at the distance of the safety margin will control rod orientation. The rods can be fed without any danger of their falling.

- Even though rods may be tilted slightly as they are sent down the chute, their orientation will be controlled when they strike the first stoppers.
- When the stoppers are lowered and movement down the chute is resumed, any slight tilt will be corrected when the rods strike the next stoppers.

Frequently, when moving objects from one place to another, it is helpful to use this canal-system approach to exercise consecutive control.

The Best Way to Clean Something Is to See That It Doesn't Get Dirty in the First Place

Where machines or other items become dirty, the usual procedure is to clean them only after the dirt has accumulated. This can be a considerable chore, however. A better method is to clean objects *so that they do not get dirty*.

Take the simple case of office windows. If you wipe them every day, a rag will suffice to keep them clean. But they will not get clean if they are wiped only once a year. The job will be enormously difficult, because the windows will have to be scrubbed with solvent or scraped with razor blades. Similarly, the most effective way to clean machines or other items is to do it *constantly*.

Objects Can Adhere to One Another in a Variety of Ways

When foreign matter adhering to objects causes problems in the plant, solutions such as blowing matter off with pressurized air or removing it with brushes are often used more or less at random. In such instances, however, differences in the nature of the adhesion require us to adopt measures appropriate to the type of adhesion involved. Foreign matter may adhere to objects in various ways.

Matter lying on top of objects. Foreign matter can be easily removed by blowing it off with pressurized air.

Matter sticking to objects. In cases where oil, grease, or rubberlike substances stick to an object, merely blowing the foreign matter with pressurized air will not work very well. Either use fluids such as water or oil, or brush the foreign matter off.

In many cases, however, what is assumed to be adhesion due to oil is in fact vacuum adhesion. In such instances, pieces can be separated from one another quite simply by making a small gap between them and then blowing in air.

Matter clinging to objects. Foreign matter clinging to an object needs to be removed by wire brushing, grinding, or cutting.

Matter jammed in objects. In these cases, the surfaces clamping the foreign matter must be separated by applying some external force — by pushing them apart or by striking them.

Thus, adhesion is not as simple as it looks. Foreign matter cannot be removed effectively until suitable judgments are first made about the nature of the adhesion and appropriate measures selected.

JUDGMENT

Ideas generated by brainstorming are the product of momentary mental flashes. The function of *judgment* is to choose from among them and criticize them in order to develop plans that can actually be used. It is important at this stage to adopt an approach in which, rather than merely shooting down ideas, one tries more positively to find ways to put them into action.

Stepping Stones for Rapid Progress: Thesis, Antithesis, and Synthesis

The dialectic is a procedure for thinking.

First, a *thesis* is put forward. Then a contradictory opinion, an *antithesis*, is espoused. As long as the thesis and antithesis are advocated at the same plane of understanding, no amount of time will be sufficient to lead to a conclusion. In general, a compromise is reached by combining the two views and splitting the difference. This is the wrong way to go about things. Rather, one should discard the defects of the two arguments, adopt their good points, and develop an improvement strategy from a higher perspective. This is known as *sublimation*. For example, suppose it is proposed that to reduce inventories, deliveries should be made to the parent plant four times per day. Opposing this, an affiliated plant asserts that the plan will not work because truck-loading operations are inefficient. Continuing to express only these views (thesis and antithesis) will lead nowhere. In many cases, a compromise position would be reached in which the parties agree to deliveries twice a day. A compromise, however, is not an improvement plan.

Suppose, on the other hand, that a method of combined loading were adopted in which trucks went around to four different companies and took on one quarter of their loads at each before making a delivery:

- Stock could be reduced.
- Truck-loading efficiency would not be lowered.

This method would be a *synthesis*, in which undesirable features of both arguments are discarded and only the good points are adopted.

In this example, assuming that a company's goods had to be transported by company trucks constituted an invisible obstacle to resolution of the problem. All that was needed was to discard that assumption and consider the issues from a higher perspective.

Thus, theses and antitheses are always in opposition when we engage in discussions. Rather than continuing those discussions on the same plane and ending up with a compromise, we can ask everyone to take off their shoes, stand on the table, and from that higher perspective consider once more the possibility that some obstacle is holding things up. This will make it possible for us to think up better plans for improvement.

Only Sham Engineers Conclude That Things Are Impossible

Whenever we want to make improvements in a production

plant, some engineers will maintain with closely reasoned arguments that the task is impossible. These are sham engineers. Indeed, one might liken them to the ministers of certain foreign nations and refer to them as "*nyet* engineers."

In contrast, there are engineers who transcend what is thought to be impossible and who are intent on success. These are true engineers.

It's the easiest thing in the world to argue logically that something is impossible. Much more difficult is to ask how something might be accomplished, to transcend its difficulties, and to imagine how it might be made possible. I believe that the true engineer's mission is to meet the challenge bravely, to go all out in pursuit of ways to do the impossible.

The Most Correct Reasoning Comes After Repeated Trials and Ultimate Success

The world is full of negative reasoning — reasoning that ignores actual trials and arrives at the conclusion that things "aren't possible" or "won't work." Yet, in many cases, surprising success is achieved by trying out things thought to be impossible. The most powerful weapon for bringing about improvement is a willingness to try. Even with the most splendid logical reasoning behind it, impossibility arguments never lead to progress. In a correctly reasoned approach, a solution is discovered in the course of trying out various possibilities.

Count Your Difficulties

Often when I visit a plant where there is some problem, I make a suggestion or two as to how things might be done. The response? "Well, that's a little difficult."

"What do you mean by 'difficult'?" I reply. "Name six problems that are making things difficult."

Oddly enough, the person I am speaking to often reels off six problems. We then discuss them one by one and nearly always come up with solutions. The point is that, rather than saying somewhat vaguely that things are "difficult," it is better to clarify difficult elements using concrete terms. Improvements can be made with unexpected ease when these difficult points are demolished one by one.

In short, avoiding vague talk about "difficulties" and expressing problems in a concrete and clear way make an effective shortcut to discovering solutions.

If the Results Are No Good, Doubt the Premises

In visiting production plants where defects are occurring, I am given many reasons why those defects should not exist:

- "Our materials are all up to specifications."
- "We maintain our machines well."
- "Our workers adhere to standard operations."

Yet if defects are actually occurring, then the facts are indisputable. Since the claim is that defects "should" not occur, we are compelled to suspect that something is amiss with that word, *should*. In other words, we have to go back to our premises and thoroughly examine them with the suspicion that something is wrong. When we do, we are liable to discover unexpected problems:

- Materials have the same labels, but they come from different manufacturers.
- Machines have been switched.
- Switching workers has meant that certain standard operations have not been adhered to.

Too often we grasp facts by guessing. In a case like this one, it is surprising how easily we can uncover the causes of problems starting with a clean slate and rethinking each premise that we used to accept unconsciously.

"Thoroughbred Experiments"

Sometimes, even though we know defects are occurring, we don't know which process is generating them or what is causing them. In this type of situation, not knowing what we don't know means the problem will never be cleared up.

An effective approach for dealing with a situation like this is to carry out a "thoroughbred experiment." For example,

1. Carefully inspect every one of 100 items being supplied as raw materials to process 1.
2. Carry out processing at process 1 using this material and then carefully inspect every one of the finished products. From these, select only acceptable items.
3. Supply only these acceptable items to process 2 and carry out processing.

Each of the resulting products is carefully inspected and only acceptable items are sent on to process 3. This procedure of carefully inspecting all products at the end of each process and then sending only acceptable items to the next process is repeated down the line. This will make clear the extent to which each process is generating defects, and the specific causes of these defects can be traced through detailed investigations of the principal processes.

Causes will never be revealed and defects will never be reduced, however, if all one does is to say vaguely that defects are causing problems. It is in such situations that I recommend that this sort of thoroughbred experiment be carried out.

If You Don't Know Why Defects Are Occurring, Make Some Defects

Sometimes in plants there are situations in which defects are occurring but their cause is unknown. In such cases, make a guess as to the most likely cause and then try to generate some defects intentionally. A comparison of the intentional defects and the previous defects will, with surprising frequency, make it possible to identify the real cause of the problem.

Rather than assuming that you must at all costs make acceptable products, experimenting on the basis of hypothetically plausible ways in which defects might occur can make it possible to trace the causes of the problem.

In any event, simply repeating that you don't know what is causing the problem will only ensure that you never know. Thinking imaginatively about problem areas, actually performing the procedure and tracking the results, and comparing the outcome with the real phenomenon are three enormously effective means for getting a grip on "unknown causes."

PROPOSAL

Improvement proposals are of no use unless they can actually be put into effect and unless they promise significant results with only modest investments. Considerable attention must always be given to so-called investment efficiency. In the next chapter, we will consider ways to implement improvement plans.

8

Stage Four: Translating Improvement Plans into Reality

The most stupendous improvement plans in the world will be ineffective unless they are translated into practice. Often at this stage the resistance of habit will prevent shop workers from implementing improvement plans. Indeed, such plans cannot be fully realized unless consent is obtained along with understanding and unless tenacious efforts are sustained.

BEFORE ANYTHING ELSE, GIVE IT A TRY

An Engineer's Instincts and a Manager's Instincts

This example involves a moisture-proofing operation in which stabilizers used in fluorescent lights were dipped in varnish, dried, and then removed. Fifty stabilizers were hung from hooks on plates and dipped into liquid varnish. Since at this stage varnish would inevitably adhere to the holes on the stabilizers from which they were hung and to the hooks, the stabilizers would stick quite firmly to the plates as they passed through the drying oven. After a worker shook the stabilizers to undo the adhesion, the stabilizers were peeled off the hooks and sent down a conveyor.

There were four sets of conveyors, and four workers were kept busy as they desperately carried out the operation of removing stabilizers one by one. When I asked the plant manager, Mr. K, why the stabilizers couldn't be removed by machine, he told me the idea wouldn't work. "The units wouldn't come off because of all the varnish stuck to them. We tried that once and the experiment failed. You've just got to have people shake the plates and then peel the stabilizers off."

"You may be right," I said, "but let's try it just once more." I used a suitably sized veneer board to push up and down against the stabilizers from below. Of 50 stabilizers, only 35 came off. "You see," said the plant manager, "it just doesn't work."

"Look," I replied, "didn't 35 of the units come off? You seem to be concerned that not all 50 came off, that 15 were left on. But if you can remove 35 stabilizers automatically by using air cylinders and the installing of a vibrating pusher, then only 15 stabilizers are left to be removed manually. At that rate, you could have a single worker handle two lines and cut down on labor costs.

"The point here is that when you say the idea won't work, you're talking about an all-or-nothing proposition. But isn't it all right to remove 35 of the stabilizers even if you can't take them all off? Rather than using your engineer's instincts and assuming that every last item has to be removed, why not use your manager's instincts and recognize the advantages of being able to remove at least some of the items?"

After I had had my say, a mechanical removal device was installed that saved the work of two people. Later on, improvements stemming from an investigation into the shape of the hooks eliminated human labor entirely and achieved a considerable cost reduction.

Thus, surprising as it may seem, a manager with the temperament of an engineer may be spellbound by technical perfection and neglect to use his instincts as a manager when thinking about improvement.

Do Humans Work Faster?

In my visits to production plants I often hear workers grumbling that management prefers mechanization even though humans work faster.

A production engineer once told me his firm had mechanized a hole-drilling operation, but the people in the plant wouldn't use the machine. They said that, although a human worker could do the job in 20 seconds per item, the automatic machine took 30 seconds. This meant that the human could process 180 items per hour, whereas the machine could handle only 120 items. "So," they concluded, "we ought to have humans do it."

I visited the plant and observed that, indeed, a human worker could process one item in 20 seconds and at 30 seconds per item, an

automatic machine took longer because of the interlock time between each operation. This was precisely why the shop foreman
wouldn't use the machine — he maintained that it was useless because humans worked faster.

At this point, I asked the production engineer how much
machines like this cost to make. He told me that they were extremely
inexpensive — only ¥ 300,000 ($1,000) each — because they were
assembled in-house, and only the parts were purchased from the outside. They were, moreover, of relatively simple construction:

1. Parts are lined up in a magazine.
2. A pusher pushes them out, where they are secured in a jig
   and drilled.
3. Parts that have been drilled are then automatically expelled.

"All right," I said to the foreman, "when I look at the job being
done, there seems to be no question that a human worker is faster
than the machine. But look, the only thing a human has to do for the
machine is to load parts into the magazine, right? If that's the case,
then even if there's another ($1,000) machine involved, the human
worker's only job would be to load magazines and take away boxes of
finished products. Doesn't that mean that one worker could be in
charge of two machines?"

"Sure, we could do that," he replied. "And all the worker would
have to do is load the magazines and then replace the boxes of finished
products, right? There would be plenty of time for that — so much that
we could even have the worker take care of deburring the holes as well."

"With another machine," I continued, "a single worker's output — given, say, 30 seconds per item for each machine — would be
240 items. That means that with another ¥600,000 ($2,000) in-
vested in two machines you will have upped productivity by 33 percent. In the end, you'll have cut costs!"

The foreman agreed that was a more profitable approach. He arranged for another machine to be made and for a single worker to op-
erate the two machines at the same time.

People on the shop floor often tend to look at the job in front of
them and conclude that a machine is useless because humans are faster. In fact, however, even if a machine takes a bit more time, as long as
the investment is modest, ultimate costs can be reduced by building
another machine and thereby increasing human productivity.

Per-item processing speed is not all there is to the problem here. The important lesson is that we consider issues like this from a higher vantage point by asking which alternative would more effectively cut costs.

Table Engineers and Catalogue Engineers

When Yang Ping-Ken, the president of Hsintung Plastics, made a rare visit to Japan, I went to see him in his Tokyo hotel room. "It's good to see you," I said. By the way, how are the fellows who took my IE course last year getting along?"

"Oh, they're doing fine," Mr. Yang replied. "As a matter of fact, now that they've taken your course, my company doesn't have any more 'table engineers'."

"Table engineers? What are they?"

"You see, it used to be that every time a problem came up, the technical people would sit around a table in the conference room and toss opinions back and forth at one another. They would all be persuaded by whoever was most aggressive or most skilled at sounding reasonable, and in the end that person's views determined the decision. They tended to be very good at coming to conclusions around a conference table.

"Since attending your course, though, they have turned into 'specific-ists': they want to check the specific facts on the shop floor or actually test specific procedures in the shop. Whenever discussions get a little complex, they go to the shop either to see which view is correct, or to run simple experiments.

"Conference-table arguments are no longer good enough. The views of engineers with practical knowledge prevail now and meetings are shorter. In addition, less time goes by before we see actual results. That's why I use the term 'table engineers' to refer to engineers who trade opinions around the conference table without ever making an effort to go into the shop."

"I get it," I said. "Now that you mention it, we have table engineers in Japan, too."

Then Mr. Yang continued his story.

"There's another kind of engineer that gives us trouble — 'catalogue engineers.' Those are engineers who collect various catalogues, look through them to find suitable machines, and then ask the company president to buy the machines. When the machines are purchased and prove to be successful, the engineers strut about triumphantly. The only talent these people have is for collecting catalogues; they never come up with new ideas of their own.

"Recently though, they've been coming up with ideas by themselves and then having the company's machine shop build machines for them. These machines may not look as stylish as commercial models, but they're far more efficient and can be built very inexpensively. If something goes wrong, they can be repaired immediately, so we no longer have to put up with broken machines sitting around for weeks at a time.

"Our technical people have gained considerable confidence recently, and the fact that about 30 percent of the machines in the plant are made in-house has not only improved efficiency, it has also improved company performance significantly. Defects have decreased and there are fewer breakdowns."

There is no question that commercial machines are fine when they are used the way everyone else uses them. Machine manufacturers, however, do not make machines that are appropriate for the particular purposes of specific companies. If you insist on asking for special capabilities, they will charge astronomical prices to accommodate you. You must design and build machines perfectly matched to your plant's tasks. It is important for engineers to take pride in the fact that they know better than anyone how to manufacture your plant's products.

THE POSITIVE POWER OF EXECUTION

IE (industrial engineering) generates improvement plans based on waste found in an investigation of the status quo. By contrast, the work-design approach starts from zero in dealing with materials costs and labor costs. It allows two kinds of expenditures in the course of developing improvement plans: unavoidable materials costs and minimal labor costs. The proponents of work design claim that their approach is by far less costly than IE, since, without exception, work-design improvement plans are less expensive than IE improvement plans.

To be sure, this claim tends to be borne out: only lukewarm improvement plans can be developed when — while identifying areas for improvement — we make compromises with the status quo. A better approach — involving deburring, for example — would be to make things so that burrs did not show up in the first place. Surprisingly good ideas will result if one asks, for example, why burrs appear at all. Burrs do not show up where a tool enters the material; they appear as the tool leaves.

If you saw through three stacked boards, burrs will show up only on the bottom board; no burrs will appear on the top two boards. This is because there is resistance below the top two boards; the saw leaves them after having cut all the way through. On the other hand, there is no resistance below the third board, so the saw catches the material before having cut all the way through, and this generates burrs.

The tool cannot cut adequately if it leaves the material at full cutting force, but if there were less of a margin for it to cut into, the tool would cut cleanly through the material before exiting. For this reason, providing a curved surface at the site where the tool exits and cutting a little bit at a time will keep burrs from forming. (See Figure 7).

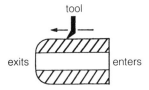

FIGURE 7. **Avoiding Burrs**

Our typical approach to deburring is to find ways to remove burrs quickly and cleanly. We must come up instead with methods for preventing burrs from occurring in the first place.

Similarly, Omark Industries set for itself the lofty objective of cutting stock to a tenth of the current figure. Omark's annual report details improvements that included the following:

- Machine layout was changed from the old homogeneous arrangement by machine type to a common process alignment arrangement that follows the flow of product processes. As a result of this improvement, and of the strict enforcement of one-piece flows, Omark was able to cut a production period of three weeks down to a mere two days.

- The sweeping implementation of SMED improvements allowed the company to reduce setup times from four hours to two minutes and forty seconds.

Everyone participated in working on these improvements, says the report, and as a result, Omark succeeded in cutting inventories by 94 percent.

Here again, this dramatic success was not brought about by bit by bit improvements through the discovery of waste inherent in current practices. Rather, it is the result of setting bold objectives, completely reforming past habits of perception, and working with the cooperation of all.

Fighting with Your "Backs to the Water"

When I visited the Y Automobile Company in 1969, the head of the auto body division told me that setups on a Schiller 1,000-ton press were taking four hours. At Volkswagen in West Germany, however, setups on the same machine only took two hours. "Mr. N, our managing director," he said, "has demanded that we find some way to do better than Volkswagen, so somehow I'd like some improvements to be made."

We first separated internal and external setup operations and then streamlined procedures in both areas. Six months later, this had made it possible to perform setups in one hour and a half, and everyone was happy.

A month after this success had been achieved, I visited Y Automobile again. This time, the auto body division head told me that Mr. N's new instructions were to cut setup time on the same 1,000-ton press down to three minutes! For a moment I was speechless. It took six months of hard work, I thought, to reduce setup times from four hours to an hour and a half. To cut them now to three minutes is impossible! But then inspiration began working.

Recently we had improved setup times for engine beds on an open-sided planer at the shipyard in Hiroshima. The point there was that we shifted what had been done during internal setup to external setup. I suddenly comprehended the most significant conceptual revolution involved in the SMED idea: take procedures that everyone assumes have to be performed during internal setup and shift them to external setup.

With the cooperation of engineers from Y Automobile, we succeed within three months in attaining setup times of three minutes.

It is all very well to demand that four-hour setups be cut in half, but what on earth did Mr. N have in mind when he demanded that setups already cut to an hour and a half be further shortened to three minutes — one-thirtieth of the previous time? Unable to fathom his real intentions, I had Mr. Akiyama, a close friend of Mr. N's and the president of S Automobile, ask Mr. N what he had been thinking. Mr. Akiyama reported to me that in response to my question, Mr. N had said: "My friend, in three minutes a man can walk 200 meters."

The response left me unsatisfied. This time, learning that a delegation from the French automobile maker Citrœn was to meet with Mr. N, I had them ask him why he thought to have the setups cut to three minutes. This time he answered in the following way: "I always like to cut things in half. For instance, I give instructions for production time to be cut in half. People are always surprised at first, but even so they come up with various ideas and work hard at them. In the meantime, I constantly visit the shop and ask how things are going. Progress is slow at first, but sooner or later someone comes up with a really superb idea and the pace begins to pick up. Eventually production time is cut in half.

"At that point, I thank everyone for their efforts, but in three months or so I give instructions for the new production period to be cut in half. This proves to be more difficult than the last time, but eventually we succeed in cutting the time in half.

"It's funny. People don't think of cutting an hour and a half to an hour as much of a goal, but if you tell them to cut the time to three minutes, then you put them in a desperate state and they come out with real resourcefulness."

What Mr. N seemed to want to say was that if you provide people with timid goals, all they will come up with are run-of-the-mill ideas — for instance, to tighten bolts with a nut runner rather than by hand. But if you give them overwhelming goals — for example, to secure objects without using threaded fastenings at all — they will think of completely new methods, such as using an interlocking system.

Later, I spoke to the delegation from Citrœn.

"I gather that you have just visited the Y Automobile company. It won't mean very much, though, if all you have done is to observe improvements superficially. Those improvements spring from the extraordinary faith and zeal of leaders, but more than that, the success you see today was only brought about through the tireless efforts of workers in the plant.

"Let me tell you a story. In the Sengoku period in Japanese history, there was a battle between the forces of the Tokugawa and the Takeda clans. The Tokugawa forces numbered only 3,000, as opposed to 10,000 Takeda soldiers, and some of the outnumbered Tokugawa troops retreated, frightened by the size of the enemy force.

"This move induced other troops to do likewise, and the entire army crumbled and pulled back. At this point, the great general Tokugawa Ieyasu skillfully guided his troops toward the banks of a wide river. If they retreated further, they would drown. With the enemy's massive army attacking from the front, death in battle was inevitable. The Tokugawa soldiers knew they were going to die and they reasoned that it was better to die fighting the enemy. So they battled like madmen, heedless of death, and contrary to all expectation, they routed the great Takeda army of 10,000.

"In Japan the Tokugawa army's predicament is referred to as *haisui no jin*, which means troops arrayed with their backs to the water.

"In a similar position, people will fight like madmen and accomplish what is generally thought to be impossible. The striking success attained at Y Automobile came because people strove hard when their backs were to the water.

"None of us can bring about a revolution with ordinary efforts. First-rate results cannot be achieved unless people are given the sort of goals that put their backs to the water and unless extraordinary efforts are put forth. I want you all to plant this idea firmly in your minds before you return to France."

As a sequel to this story, I am told that the untranslated Japanese phrase *haisui no jin* is still often heard at Citroën.

How About Doing It Tomorrow?

This is a story from my childhood.

A man wanting a haircut goes to a barbershop and sees a sign posted outside that reads "Free Haircuts Tomorrow."

"Free haircuts tomorrow?" the man thinks. "I'd miss out if I got one today."

The next day he returns to the barbershop and the sign is still there: "Free Haircuts Tomorrow." Once again, he decides to wait. The following day the same sign is up and in the end, of course, the man lives the rest of his life without getting his hair cut.

The point is that human beings rely on tomorrow even more than on God or other people. Yet for people who believe in tomorrow, tomorrow never comes. People who always intend to get things done tomorrow end up never being able to do anything as long as they live.

In another well-known fable, a baby skylark says to its mother, "We have to move our nest because the farmer who owns this field of wheat has asked his neighbors to reap the wheat tomorrow."

"Don't worry," the mother replies, and they do not move.

The next day, the baby skylark tells its mother that the farmer has come and said that the neighbors would not come because they were all busy. "The farmer said he had no choice but to have his relatives help reap the wheat tomorrow," says the baby skylark. "We have to move!"

"Don't worry," his mother says, and shows not the slightest sign of moving.

The following day, the baby skylark says, "Mother, today the farmer came and said that his relatives had found some reason or other not to help him. He said he had no choice but to ask his children."

"There's nothing to worry about," the mother says, and still they do not move.

The day after that, the baby skylark says, "Today the farmer came again and he said that his children were all heartless. 'They come out with some excuse or other and won't lend me a hand. At this rate, I'll miss the season for reaping. I guess *tomorrow I'll have to do it myself!*' "

When the mother hears this news, she declares that they must move the nest right away.

Everyone tends to want to rely on others, but things don't get moving that way. The job cannot be done unless you lead the way and do it yourself.

At Y Automobile, Mr. N tells me:

"Whenever I ask the fellows in purchasing why some item we ordered is late, they say that they've reminded the supplier. Then I ask whether they've checked to see how much headway has been made on the problem. Whoever is in charge of the order at the supplier's has told them over the telephone that he'll take care of it, they say. They have confidence in him.

"But this is all wrong. I'm always nagging my people, telling them that the items they've ordered will never be delivered on time unless they're ready to go in person to the supplier and check out the facts for themselves — to plant themselves on the supplier's doorstep if need be. The problem is that they don't do what I tell them to."

Somehow, when I hear Mr. N's story, I can't help but wonder if those suppliers of his might be the kind who would believe they can get a free haircut tomorrow.

The Same as Yesterday Isn't Good Enough

Sometimes when I visit companies, I find people who say "no" to improvement plans from the start. "After all," they say, "we've been doing things this way for ten years and never had any problems. Everything's fine."

"I see," I say for the sake of politeness, but underneath I want to ask them if they really have made no progress in ten years.

Human beings cannot progress unless somehow they do things differently today from the way they did them yesterday.

To be sure, there is a sort of peace of mind that comes of doing things the traditional way if that way has led to a certain degree of success. It is perfectly natural that doing new things is accompanied by certain risks.

But there will never be any progress made if yesterday's methods are used forever. You have to try out new ways of doing things. If you do, perhaps half of what you try will end in failure, but the other half will be linked to progress.

Before World War II, Japan had an enormously accomplished finance minister named Hijikata. Hijikata had graduated with a first-rate record from a teacher-training school in Kōchi Prefecture. On the occasion of his graduation, he went to pay his respects to a teacher he greatly admired. "I hope to be as great as you are," he told the teacher.

"Hijikata," the teacher admonished him, "there would never be any progress at all in the world if students were satisfied to attain the same level as their teachers. You've got to set your sights on surpassing me."

Spurred on by these words, Hijikata worked hard and went on to a higher teacher-training school. Afterward he studied economics on his own, became a politician, and achieved the distinction of becoming Minister of Finance. In his autobiography, Hijikata tells how that single counsel from his teacher changed the course of his life.

Indeed, there would be no progress in the world if students did not surpass their teachers.

Plant "Trees" Throughout the Factory

In recent years I have frequently travelled to Europe and the United States. Every time I go, I am impressed by how clean European and American factories are.

The cleanliness of the insides of buildings is part of the reason for this impression, of course. In addition, lawns and courtyards are planted with trees and are full of greenery and blooming flowers, all to please the sensibilities of the observer. Indeed, many factories give the impression of being located in the midst of a park.

Lately, perhaps as a result of foreign influence, there has been a most felicitous trend toward environmental beautification in Japan, and there is a greater number of graceful and neat industrial plants here than ever before.

For example, the president of K Metals recently participated in a number of study trips to other countries and, perhaps because of having seen attractive factories there, he has worked hard within the last two or three years to beautify his company's facilities. Visitors to K Metals are said to spare no praise in complimenting him on the firm's neat and pleasant plant.

In this same plant, however, many argumentative people have been slow to make progress on recommended improvements such as SMED or *poka-yoke*. In fact, there is a tendency to ignore such ideas altogether.

I once commented on this situation to the company's president. "You have," I said, "recently made your facilities quite attractive by planting trees and flowers. But there are more important trees that you seem to have forgotten to plant."

"More important trees?" he replied. "What do you mean?"

"I'm talking about planting trees inside the factory," I said.

"Inside the factory? What trees would I plant inside the factory?"

"Trees of will — the will to do things right."

He seemed to understand what I meant, because later, under his leadership, rapid improvements were made and considerable success was achieved.

There is no question that a beautiful exterior environment is important for an industrial plant, but even more crucial is increased efficiency inside. To achieve this, there is nothing more important than planting "trees of will."

Don't Eat Your Fifth Bowl of Rice First

This is a folktale I heard after the war when I was living in the town of Takanabe in Miyazaki Prefecture.

A certain man was climbing a mountain and got completely lost. After walking this way and that, he finally managed to find his way back home at about 3 o'clock in the afternoon. His mother had worried about him and she asked him where he had been and what had happened.

"Not now," the man answered. "Give me something to eat first; I'm starving."

One after another, he wolfed down four bowls of rice, and only when he got to the fifth bowl did his belly feel full. At this point the man cried out, "Damn! I should have eaten the fifth bowl first!"

But is there any way he could have done that? Obviously the fifth bowlful would only have made him feel full after he had eaten the first, second, third, and fourth bowls of rice.

Similarly, improvement requires five steps:

- *First bowl*: plow the field
- *Second bowl*: spread base manure
- *Third bowl*: plant seeds
- *Fourth bowl*: add additional fertilizer
- *Fifth bowl*: shoots finally appear

Or, in other words:

- Discuss the need for improvement and "set the stage."
- Hold discussions in active teams and decide to make suggestions for improvement.
- Determine broad themes of improvement.
- Hold talks on how ideas should be brought up.
- Present suggestions for improvement.

Soliciting suggestions for improvement one day does not mean suggestions will show up the next. One must never forget that the young shoots of improvement suggestions will appear only where tenacious leaders invest enthusiasm and their hard work.

Industrial engineers charged with improvement — especially young ones — are anxious to see results and they expect the fruits of improvement to ripen quickly. This does not necessarily happen, however, and some people are disappointed. Improvement does not yield fruit so simply; you have to know enough to lay the groundwork and to put in honest effort.

Otemon'ya Management

At the laboratory of a plant in Kumamoto, I once gave a talk sponsored by the local Chamber of Commerce on "Ways of Thinking for Plant Improvement." At that talk, I referred to a famous song from Kumamoto, "Otemon'ya."

"As I visit companies throughout Japan," I said, "wherever I go, I run into firms that practice 'Otemon'ya' management."

"What do you mean by Otemon'ya management?" one member of the audience asked.

"I'm talking about a system in which plans and instructions are not determined clearly and fully," I explained. "Immature plans and vague instructions are given out and the rest is left to those who implement them. The approach is described by the words of the song: '...and let the rest take care of itself.'

"Whenever some blunder or confusion occurs on the shop floor, managers ignore their own shortcomings and bawl out subordinates for being so stupid. Given the surprising number of managers who behave like this, Otemon'ya management poses a real problem. I'd like to see such practices changed for the better."

The Magic Mallet

This is an Italian fairy tale.

Three children went to the mountain to gather chestnuts. They went farther and farther into the woods until they lost their way, and after wandering in all directions, at last they entered the Land of Magic. There they met the old woman of the Land of Magic. They were all adorable children, and she treated them to every hospitality. Before they knew it, a month had gone by.

At length they grew homesick and told the old woman they wanted to go back to their own homes.

"Yes," said the old woman, "I suppose you ought to go back. Your mothers and fathers must be worrying about you. But as keepsakes of the Land of Magic, I have magic mallets for you — mallets that can give you whatever you want. Just tell me what you'd like most of all."

The first child said, "I want a mallet that can give me whatever wonderful food I want," and he was given the mallet.

The second child, when asked what he wanted, said, "a mallet that can give me any jewel I might want." The old woman gave him a mallet that would do just that.

Then the old woman asked the third child what he wanted from his mallet. He thought a moment, and then said, "Well, I'd like a mallet that would give me whatever I wanted." The old woman gave him his mallet.

Now, which child was the cleverest?

The Nihon Pulp company is located in the town of Nichinan in southern Kyūshū. I learned from a newspaper article that Mr. S, the head of the company's Engineering Division, had invented a revolutionary device for refining pulp. Since I had business at Nihon Pulp, I arranged to meet with Mr. S for lunch. I told him that I had heard of his remarkable device and asked him how he came to invent it. This was his reply:

"I graduated from Kyoto Imperial University and N, my closest friend from those days, was the chief engineer at a tannery in Himeji. Whenever I traveled to Tokyo or Osaka, I always took a sleeper back to Nichinan in the hope that I could stop off in Himeji and see my friend, but a suitable opportunity never presented itself.

"By chance, however, once when I had an appointment with an important client in Osaka, the party I was to meet was unexpectedly held up by the arrival of a visitor from abroad and he asked to postpone our meeting for a day. This gave me a free day in Osaka — a perfect chance, I told myself, to see my old friend; so right away I went down to Himeji to visit N at the tannery.

"We greeted one another warmly and chatted on and on about the old days. Presently N asked me if I would like to see his tannery. I refused, saying that his plant was entirely different from anything I was familiar with and that, first of all, a tannery would probably stink and be dirty. Nothing, I said, would be gained by my seeing it.

"My friend urged me not to prejudge the plant. 'Just have a look around,' he said. Reluctantly, I let him show me the plant. He showed me various machines and then we came to a process involving a completely different kind of machinery.

" 'What does that apparatus do?' I asked my friend.

" 'It's a device for washing hides,' he replied.

"I asked him what principle it worked on and as I listened to his explanation, it occurred to me that the same type of device could be used for refining pulp. Afterward I studied the problem from various angles and invented a revolutionary pulp-refining device.

"I had visited other paper manufacturers such as Ōji Paper, Jūjō Paper, and Honshū Paper any number of times, but they all ran pretty much the same kind of operation as we did and I hadn't learned much. When I observed the tannery — a completely different industry — and studied the principles involved, I realized that even though their devices looked different, they could be applied to pulp production. Nowadays I make a point of visiting innovative plants in a variety of industries."

After I heard this story, it seemed to me that Mr. S had come back from the Land of Magic carrying a mallet that could produce anything. Apparently, he had learned more than just know-how; he had learned know-why as well. It occurred to me that Mr. S had worked as hard as he had because he went beyond the external appearance of the apparatus and actively grasped the principles of its construction.

At N Woodworking, I met with the company president, Mr. Ōmizu, over lunch. "Dr. Shingo," he told me, "I was deeply impressed by your story about the head engineer at Nihon Pulp. Until now, I have tried mainly to visit woodworking companies, but some companies aren't willing to have me visit, and I don't get much out of seeing the firms I can visit.

"Recently, though, I have changed my approach and have actively made a point of visiting companies in other fields — machine industries and casting or forging companies. It's fairly easy to get permission to see companies like that. What's more, I have them explain the principles behind their equipment and not just the superficial manufacturing methods. This has given me more useful hints than I would ever have thought possible. Within the past year, in fact, we've built about ten machines of types that none of our competitors have. To keep this going, we are constantly trying to follow your advice about striving to get a grip on know-why as well as know-how.

"Copying what our competition was doing would mean that we'd always have to content ourselves with being a second-rate company. I understand now that observing what goes on in different kinds of plants is a far more effective way for ours to become a first-rate, quality company."

Like Mr. S, Mr. Ōmizu had come back from the Land of Magic carrying a mallet that could produce anything.

Don't Use the Same Slogan for the Foreman and the Company President

Whenever a new policy for improving efficiency comes out, some Japanese companies make up a slogan to announce the president's plans. If the company president's slogan is "Reduce Inventory!" then division heads and department chiefs will take up the same cry and group leaders and foremen will similarly issue calls for inventory reduction.

But this isn't the way things should work. If a company president makes an appeal to "Reduce Inventory!" the division heads and department heads should adopt a more concrete policy, like "Shorten setup times throughout, in order to carry out small-lot production!"

Next, the group leaders and foremen need to translate this into an even more specific slogan that shop workers will immediately understand: "Standardize all die heights and clamping surface thicknesses!"

If this isn't done, the same slogan will be chanted like a meaningless litany all the way down the chain of command and solid results will be few and far between.

Fair Weather Always Follows the Rain

I joined the First Kurume Tank Corps in 1931, a time when we might have been sent into battle at any moment. Our training instructor, a Lieutenant Harada, made a profound impression on me that has lasted to this day.

"From this instant on," he told us, "you may be sent into battle at any moment. When you do move onto the battlefield, sometimes things will go well for our side and you will be on the offensive. At other times you will be surrounded by powerful enemy forces and will be obliged to take defensive measures and persevere until reinforcements arrive.

"Everything will go fairly smoothly for you when you are battling from a position of strength. The problem will come when you are holding out patiently in a defensive position. In such a situation, those of you who are weak of spirit may be seized by fear and rush wildly out of the trenches. The enemy will be waiting for you, and you will be shot dead on the spot. Not only that, the enemy will learn our location, and the entire squad may be wiped out.

"If you find yourselves in this situation, you must be calm and never give up the hope that reinforcements will arrive. It is supremely important, moreover, that you rest and save your energies for the next offensive.

"Once a good opportunity springs out in front of you, you should run the 100 meters to the next trench and jump in. Those who hesitate and are slow to come out of the trenches, will be spotted and will end up being targets for enemy rifles.

"As you all know, fair weather always follows rain and rain always follows fair weather. Neither rain nor fair weather ever lasts uninterrupted for a year.

"I believe that life moves sort of like a wave motion and just as wave crests do not continue forever, neither do wave troughs. This is true both in battle and in life, and the attitude with which you face the troughs is extremely important."

These words have had a significant impact on my entire life ever since. When my improvement work has not gone as well as I expected, when relations with other people have turned sour, and, in particular, when I have fallen ill, I think, "Aha! This is the trough of a wave; this is life's rainy season. Fair weather will come along soon." Time and time again, this thought has dispelled my impatience and restored my sense of equilibrium.

On a visit to Y Automobile, I met someone who had attended my IE course five years earlier, a Mr. Sametani of the Production Engineering Department. He seemed a little depressed and I asked him if he was feeling well.

"It's not that," he replied. "I just don't get along with the new department head. All he does is find fault with what I do and I'm sick of it. I just can't get excited about my job — even you noticed it."

I tried to comfort him before I left. "Listen, Mr. Sametani," I said. "Life moves in a sort of wave motion. Right now you're in a rainy season. Rather than brooding about it, you've got to recharge your batteries for the future. In other words, do some studying or make what improvements you can and get to know the people on the shop floor. Believe me, if you take an interest in something and turn yourself around, fair weather will show up before long."

When I went back to Y Automobile after about a year I sought out Mr. Sametani. This time he was full of energy and in high spirits. When I asked him how things were going, he thanked me vigorously. "What you told me really snapped me out of it," he said. "Fortunately the new department head really dotes on me, and I'm working in top form. It's just like you said. Fair weather always follows the rain."

To digress a bit, I have always felt that, rather than berating our spouses for dawdling when they are struggling with a job and stuck in the trough of one of life's waves, we should provide the protective psychological support needed to tide them over to the next wave crest so that together we can look forward to sunnier days. Indeed, I find it profoundly telling that the Japanese written character for "person" depicts two individuals helping one another:

Defensive Territories

One of the directors of Y Automobile told me the following story:

"Universities nowadays are teaching nothing but theories — theories of organization, and ideas about responsibility and authority, and so on. Managers end up thinking of these as sacred principles. They seem to forget that organization means an arrangement for running a business efficiently.

"Their organization theories say that if a baseball game were to begin right now, the infielders would get together and confer. They might agree on various things: the defensive boundary between first base and second base, the defensive boundary between second base and the shortstop, the defensive boundary between the shortstop and third base. If a grounder came rolling out, each infielder would ascertain which side of the boundary the ball was on and stand by and watch if it wasn't on his side. Many theories of organization are like this.

"In a game, the significant thing is winning, not deciding whose territory the ball is going to roll into. When it's hard to tell which side of the line the ball is going to end up on, or when one player is in a better position, even though the ball is not in his territory, it seems to me that the most important thing is to go for the ball — even if you bump into your teammate — and to throw it to first base to get the hitter out.

"Of course, not having any standards at all would result in confusion, so defensive territories should be staked out in a general way. The problem is that since the crucial thing is winning, it's clearly wrong to give precedence to the mechanical guarding of defensive territories.

"I find it annoying that so many managers claim I am 'overstepping my authority' or 'exceeding my responsibilities' if I call attention to issues concerning work in departments other than my own. Of course, when I do, I still have to get in touch afterward with whomever is nominally in charge.

"At any rate, even outside the realm of general organization theory, urging people to come up with ideas to benefit the company is not particularly well thought of."

Fortunately, the atmosphere at Y Automobile was such that opinions poured forth without regard to the company's organization. Indeed, it was impressive to see how truly lively the environment inside the company was.

It may be important to adhere to formal organizational charts, yet there are many issues to consider. For example, would it be better to deviate from the organization a bit and let everyone show what he or she can do?

As I go around from one company to another, how often I hear managers respond to problems that have been raised with, "That's not in my jurisdiction!"

9

Understanding and Conviction

Understanding Alone Isn't Enough to Get People Moving

People will understand something if the reasoning is explained to them. But understanding by itself will never get things put into practical operation. People will not swing into action until they are convinced by the arguments.

Understanding is a function of reason, whereas *conviction* is an emotion. We may very well deal with someone's new idea by saying, "What that guy says is correct, but I'm not going to do it because I don't like him." We may believe that demolishing someone with logic will get him to do what we want, but in fact, using arguments to overwhelm people often has the opposite effect.

People will not be set in motion until they are convinced on an emotional level based on trust — until they can say, "That's right! I know that'll make the job easier and improve quality at the same time!" or "It looks kind of hard, but I believe the guy who's telling me this, so it's got to work!"

For example, in an effort to improve a setup operation at T Auto Body, the head of the Production Engineering section made measurements of the operation and indicated various areas for improvement, but these suggestions never seemed to be put into practice. At this point, the department head, Mr. Yamaguchi, suggested that the setup operation be videotaped and then that the videotape be shown to the workers when the setup was completed. When the workers saw the tape, they came out with all sorts of observations ("You mean I do *that*?" "We sure spend a lot of time looking for tools." "Why the delays?"), and improvements made right away cut setup time in half.

In the end, then, the workers didn't really believe the Production Engineering representative when he told them what he had ob-

129

served. They insisted that delays were not much of a problem or that they didn't behave as the production engineer claimed they did. Actually seeing themselves and watching their own movements on the videotape convinced them, however, and they quickly took action to remedy the situation.

I still remember what Mr. Yamaguchi told me about the experience at the time. "People can't see themselves from the back," he said, "so even if someone tells them that there is a dirty spot there, they tend not to believe it. But if they see the spot themselves on videotape, they will be convinced and will move quickly to deal with the problem."

Thus, people tend not to swing into action on the strength of the logic of some new idea. Putting new ideas into effect demands, above all else, that the people involved be *convinced*.

It is crucial, also, to understand that being convinced of something is a function of emotion rather than of reason. The observation that "people cannot see themselves from the back" is an apt one, indeed.

A Two-Step Method of Persuasion

S Manufacturing Company makes plastic home electronics products. On a visit to the parent company in Osaka, the president of S Manufacturing was asked to increase output by 30 percent within three months.

As soon as he got back to Tokyo, the president called a meeting of division and department heads. "Yesterday," he told them, "our parent company, A Television, asked us to raise production output by 30 percent within the next three months. I'd like us all to talk about what steps we should take to achieve this."

He had no sooner made this announcement than the head of the plant's Manufacturing Department volunteered the opinion that he would need three more machines installed.

"All right," the president replied.

Then the head of the Management Department spoke up: "We'll have to have three shifts, so with three people each shift, that will mean getting nine people.

"I see," said the president.

The head of the Inspection Department added that he would need more inspectors and the head of the Finishing Department said,

"We'll need more workers for finishing and also, we're short on space even now, so we'll have to have a new operations area built."

One after another, people from each department asked for more equipment, more people, or more space.

To everyone, the president nodded and said, "I see" or "Uh-hm." About an hour later, when everyone's opinions had been thoroughly aired, he suggested that they take a short break. For the next ten minutes, they all drank coffee and made small talk.

When the meeting started up again the president addressed the group: "I listened to what you all had to say earlier, and I must say, I sympathize with your requests — they all seem quite reasonable to me. As you know, though, this plant is located in the middle of a residential area and people's houses come right up to our wall. We might be able to buy more equipment or add workers, but I regret to point out that there's simply no more space available on our plot of land. I realize this is probably asking the impossible, but I wonder if there isn't some way to increase output with the space and the machines we have currently available to us."

Everyone fell glumly silent at this and not a word was spoken for two or three minutes. Suddenly, the head of the Engineering Department asked, "What's the work rate for our current machines, anyway?"

"About 65 percent," the Manufacturing Department head replied.

"And what accounts for the largest portion of the remaining 35 percent?"

"Well, that would have to be setup time. We've been getting a lot of small-lot orders from our parent company recently, and the number of setups we have to perform has risen about 30 percent."

"About how long does a setup take now?"

"I'd say about one hour."

"Look, our parent company has been recommending for about six months now that we implement single-minute exchange of die. How about giving it some thought? The word is that one of our sister firms, the M Company, reduced its setups to around eight minutes."

"That's true," said the Manufacturing Department chief. "We should definitely give it a try."

At that point, the head of the Engineering Department spoke up and suggested looking into applying SMED to vacuum forming right away. He had heard, he said, that it might eliminate deburring completely and cut the defect rate by four-fifths. The company president added, "If we can directly link the forming process and the finishing process, we can cut down on inventory and free up some space."

"How about hooking up finishing with the packaging process as well?" someone suggested.

"And we could use ultrasonic waves to disconnect the gates." said someone else.

The atmosphere had changed completely. Innovative ideas came pouring forth. A number of these ideas were in fact put into effect, with the result that three months later, a 27 percent increase in real output was achieved without the addition of either machines or workers.

There can be no doubt that the environment from which these changes sprang could never have taken hold if the company president had immediately countered everyone's views with, "No, we can't do that. We can't make the plant any bigger so it won't work. You ought to know that." It seems to me that the president's success lay in a two-step method of persuasion. At first he nodded and let people with opposing views express them fully; then, when they had emptied their brains, he took a new tack and had everyone think of more innovative ideas.

It is an impressive approach, one that makes it possible to grasp the oblique strands of people's thoughts.

The Magic Words "I See What You Mean"

At a tobacco processing plant, I once suggested that each package of cut tobacco be sent down a chute and onto a conveyor as soon as it was glued and sealed. The proposal was immediately rejected: "It won't work because the glue won't hold."

What had to be decided at this point was whether the objection was frontal or whether it was essentially cautionary. Resolving such questions demands winning time, and in situations like this, time can be won by using the magic words "I see what you mean."

The phrase indicates neither agreement nor disagreement; it is neutral and says only, "Yes, that's true." While you are saying, "I see what you mean," you should be scrutinizing your listener's counterargument and if, in spite of its negative tone, you find it to be essentially cautionary, then you should accept it.

Your "I see what you mean" may give a hostile listener the impression that he has gotten you to accept his assertions and in that sense it acts as a psychological neutralizing agent, for the atmosphere surrounding the subsequent exchange will have been changed from one of debate to one of discussion.

If you challenge people with the accusation that they do nothing but object, exchanges will flare into emotional debates, and in the end, satisfactory conclusions will be unattainable. With "I see what you mean," you can take in what your interlocutor says and, if his objection is essentially cautionary, you can agree that you have overlooked something and then address the issue. This non-confrontational, affirmative approach is an effective way to develop better improvement plans. The fact is that most people on the shop floor tend to oppose improvement schemes. The liberal use of neutralizing phrases such as "I see what you mean" and "that's true" will change the atmosphere from one of debate to one of discussion, and this is extremely effective in implementing improvements.

Ninety-nine Percent of Objections Are Cautionary

The cut-tobacco packaging operation mentioned above consisted of several repeated motions:

- Apply glue to the right edge of the packaging paper and glue the package shut.
- Line up five sealed packages of tobacco on the left.
- Take up groups of five packages and, reaching out, place them on the conveyor.

When I suggested to the plant manager that a chute could be used to send each package to the conveyor as soon as it is sealed, he rejected the proposal outright: "It won't work because the glue won't hold. Amateurish ideas like that don't work out."

I thought about this for a bit. The point of my improvement was that:

- Fully extending the arm to reach out to the conveyor is wasteful.
- It is annoying to have to think about how many packages have been completed.
- The rhythm of movement in the task is interrupted by the intrusion of a different movement every five items.

Yet there was really no objection to these issues. The objection was simply that the idea was no good because the glue would not hold.

In effect, I felt, the objection was unjustified, because it was an objection to a *means* and not to the *goals* of the improvement. Since all that was needed was to make sure the glue held, I experimented to see how much drying was required. Differences in chutes were negligible and I knew that the glue would dry in the time it took to prepare five packages, so I made a suggestion:

- When gluing and sealing on the first package is complete, set that package to the left.
- When the second package is complete, place it to the left, pushing the first package over.
- Continue pushing the row of packages over as each new one is completed and the sixth package will fall into the chute and onto the conveyor.

This worked beautifully.

The manager had protested that the idea would not work because the glue would not hold. Yet suppose he had said, "That's a good idea, but you'll have to give some thought to whether the glue will hold"? If he had, his view would clearly have been cautionary. Thus, by changing the way the view is expressed, pointing out that the glue will not hold becomes either an objection or a piece of cautionary advice.

Even if the tone of voice is confrontational, the content of an objection is often cautionary, so we must entertain that possibility. There is no doubt that the whole idea would have fallen on its face if I had responded to the manager's objection by ignoring what he had to say.

I suggest to you that 99 percent of all objections are cautionary. The words used tend to determine whether the response is a warning or an objection, but the basic content is nearly always cautionary. The remaining 1 percent of cases most likely involve some sort of misapprehension or hostility.

No matter what the tone of an objection, seize the essence of what is being said, use it to offset the weakness in your suggestion, and develop a better proposal.

Ninety-nine Percent of What We Say Is for the Benefit of Our Listeners

Ninety-nine percent of what comes out of our mouths is for the benefit of listeners. The remaining 1 percent is when we talk to ourselves, sing in the shower, or speak just for the pleasure of admiring our own voices. Although we may realize that we speak for the sake of others, do we always speak with the clear object of making ourselves understood?

Scholars and politicians sometimes use the phrase, "national consensus," but at what percentage of public understanding is a real consensus reached? In any event, "making oneself understood" is essential for any kind of discussion, and it is important, furthermore, to verify that listeners have indeed understood.

In the military, information is sometimes transmitted to other units orally by messengers. An oral order is given: "Private Saitō, tell Takeda Company that xxxx." Private Saitō then repeats the message: "Repeat! Private Saitō is going to tell Takeda Company that xxyy."

If there is a mistake, Private Saitō is corrected ("No, not xxyy; xxxx!") and when he can repeat the message correctly he is dispatched as a messenger. Since an error in message transmission might result in the destruction of the entire unit, tremendous care is put into verifying that the recipient of the message has understood correctly.

But why wait for a war to use this idea — don't we need to apply it actively to our current jobs?

I often telephone home when I am away on business. When I go through a hotel's front desk, I ask for number 0466 22 9505. The operator says "yes, sir," and the call goes through. Thinking I am speaking to my wife, I begin to talk about what has happened during the day. Then a voice at the other end of the line says, "Excuse me, whom am I speaking to?"

Realizing at once that a mistake has been made, I apologize for the error. In many of these calls, the number goes through as 9050 instead of 9505. So now, when the operator says "yes, sir," I ask him or her to repeat the number to me. If the answer is 0466 22 9050, I have the number corrected to 0466 22 9505. Nowadays, I no longer get wrong numbers.

Twenty years ago, I ran a production technology seminar for foremen at Y Machinery. At the final round-table discussion, a fairly old foreman came up to me with a beer in his hand and said, "Your talks were very good, Dr. Shingo."

"That good?" I responded.

"I liked it that you didn't use a single word of English. And it was especially good that you talked about 'chinburo'."

Chinburo was company slang for "chain block"; I had used the term in one of my talks. Earlier quality control seminars that N had attended had been full of unfamiliar terminology, and he said he had given up on understanding them from the start. He attended three days' worth of seminars and went home without having understood a single thing. This case may be unusual, but it is extremely important for us to remember that 99 percent of what comes out of our mouths is for the benefit of our listeners.

Life Is Not an Endless Debate

In this world of ours there are many people who, despite clear thinking and an extraordinary gift for logical argumentation, are isolated because neither their subordinates nor their superiors trust them.

One morning, as I was walking through the Fujisawa train station with the intention of going to Tokyo, I chanced to run into Mr. Takabayashi of Y Machinery in Aichi Prefecture.

"Out on a business trip so early?" I asked.

"No," he replied. "Three months ago I was transferred to H Precision Works and now I'm working in Tokyo at H Machinery, one of their daughter companies. I'm just on my way to work."

"Really?" I said. "I'm headed for Tokyo, too. Let's ride together." We boarded the train and took seats next to one another.

"I haven't seen you for quite a while," I said. "How have things been going?"

"When I was head of the Manufacturing Division at Y Machinery, H Precision Works begged me to come work for them. Their daughter company, H Machinery, was losing money and the people there were fighting desperately to streamline their plant."

From this topic we moved to many others, but gradually, as Mr. Takabayashi talked about the past, his tone grew somewhat formal.

"Dr. Shingo, I attended one of your production technology seminars at Y Automobile some 15 years ago. You said something in a talk you gave then that I will never forget as long as I live. In explaining the difference between understanding and conviction, you said that life isn't an endless debate. The instant you said that, I remember stiffening a little. From that minute onward, my ideas changed."

"Really?" I said. "You mean it was that impressive?"

We moved on to a completely different subject, and we parted when Mr. Takabayashi got off the train at Shinagawa.

About half a year later, I had occasion to visit Y Machinery. After I had discussed current problems with Mr. Kurimura, the company director in charge of production, an intense expression suddenly came over his face — an expression that recalled the look Mr. Takabayashi had when he had talked about life not being an endless debate. I mentioned to Mr. Kurimura that I had run into Mr. Takabayashi, and told him what we had talked about in the train.

"You know," said Mr. Kurimura, "Takabayashi was a very bright young man with top-notch grades in school. Family circumstances prevented him from going to a university, though, and he graduated from a technical college. He was gradually promoted in the company and became a section chief, but whenever a subordinate would come to consult him, he would chew the guy out for not understanding what was going on.

"At meetings, too, he went after college-educated department heads with his arguments. You couldn't contradict him because he was usually right, so the department heads, unwilling to cross swords with him, ended up keeping quiet. People both above him and below him took a dislike to him and he ended up being isolated.

"He was judged to be unsuitable for the manufacturing shop, so when it came time for him to be promoted he was put in charge of inspection. As head of the Inspection Department, he gave the Manufacturing Department head hell whenever defects showed up and sometimes even directly criticized the head of the entire Manufacturing Division. Reason was on his side, though, and the people in charge of manufacturing couldn't rebut his charges. Everybody avoided him on the theory that it was safer not to tangle with him.

"During his tenure as head of the Inspection Department, he attended one of your production seminars, and suddenly he was a changed man. His attitude changed completely. When subordinates came to him he listened to their explanations carefully and gave them helpful suggestions or appropriate advice.

"What's more, he stopped snarling at everyone else's ideas. He appreciated the ideas of others and encouraged their further development in constructive and supportive ways. His popularity among subordinates grew and his superiors became more receptive to him. In a very short time he was chosen to be Manufacturing Division head.

"When H Precision Works asked us to send over someone of 'top-notch executive caliber,' there was unanimous agreement at an executive meeting that Takabayashi would be perfect for the job."

Perhaps Mr. Takabayashi took delight in attacking others because he secretly resented university graduates; perhaps he took unconscious pride in his own intelligence. He was an intelligent man, however, and when he heard the lecture about the difference between understanding and conviction, his whole attitude seems to have changed. He realized that the real goal was not to attack others with logic, but to convince people of good ideas and to get them to put those ideas into effect successfully. Life is not an endless debate, indeed!

Here is another story.

In an evening feedback session at the conclusion of one of my IE courses, a Mr. Kimura from A Electric Company's Tsukamoto plant stood up with a dreadfully serious look on his face and said, "This course has changed my view of life. That's all I have to say." Then he sat back down.

It was such an abrupt declaration that on a visit to the Tsukamoto plant some six months later, I told the story to Mr. Ōbayashi, the head of the Operations Division. "Really?" said Mr. Ōbayashi. "That brings a story to mind.

"Kimura's grades at school were extraordinarily high, but his family was poor and he was able to graduate only from a technical high school.

"He was a manager at the time I am speaking of and was difficult for subordinates to talk to. Without waiting to hear all of what they had to say, he looked for faults in their suggestions and really chewed them out. Even at production meetings, he seized on mistakes that department heads made and beat them over the heads with logic. Everyone ostracized him for this and he ended up isolated.

"From the minute he came back from the IE course, Kimura began to listen carefully to what subordinates had to say and to offer suitable advice. It came to be known that problems could be resolved by consulting the manager. At production meetings, too, we all changed our minds about him because he listened to other people's views and then offered first-rate, constructive plans to follow. Within three months, he was chosen to direct the plant's branch of the labor union."

Mr. Kimura was soon promoted to department head and five

years later he became plant manager.

Here again is someone who realized that the purpose is not to demolish other people with arguments, but to convince people of the value of new ideas and to get results by putting those ideas into action. Surely the attainment of this higher purpose is what Mr. Kimura referred to when he declared that his "view of life" had changed.

In any case, I want to remind all the superior intellects in the world that life is not an endless debate.

Put Your Conclusions First

During plant visits I often ask about the outcome of problems we have discussed on my previous trips.

"Oh, that? Well, we did this and then we did this." The entire process is explained to me, and then I am told either, "we finally reached our goal" or "the problem is still there." In other words, the conclusion usually comes at the end.

As far as I am concerned as a listener, however, there is no need for me to listen particularly carefully if the problem has been solved. Conversely, if the result was unsatisfactory, I usually ask *why* things did not work out. As the explanation progresses, I note where strategic errors occurred and what points I want to look into further. To do this, I need to pay close attention to what is being said to me. If necessary, I can make suitable cautionary remarks.

If I don't hear about an unsatisfactory outcome until after the process is explained, I tend to ask for the explanation all over again because I cannot remember what strategic errors were made.

It is much more effective to have the process explained in reverse, to have problem areas clearly stated and then to have conclusions given right at the beginning. If one thinks about the reasons for explaining things, no one should find it difficult to understand that explanations that present conclusions first are considerably more expedient.

Deduction and Induction

For five hundred years after the birth of mankind, there were no "rules" whatsoever for how to talk. Then man discovered the method of *deduction*, in which a principle is explained and then specific examples are presented. For example, we present a principle: waste is a function of means rather than goals.

Then we explain it in concrete terms:

- Method A is wasteful because it involves superfluous transport.
- Unnecessary inventory accumulates in response to the occurrence of defects.

After fifteen hundred years or so had gone by, man discovered another method — *induction*.

Induction means presenting several specific examples and then explaining them in terms of some reasonable principle. In this method, everyday, concrete facts are presented and then the listener is made aware of a principle linking those facts.

For instance, one might cite several concrete examples:

- When you go to a grocery store and buy bananas, you may notice that part of what you paid for is inedible skin.
- After going to the bathroom, it is a mistake — in terms of hygiene — to wash one's hands before putting one's clothes in order.

The general principle is explained afterwards: in many everyday acts we are not conscious of being wasteful. This is an inductive explanation.

Similarly, it is more persuasive to describe how people sometimes act in illogical ways unconsciously, and then impress upon them the need to track down everyday goals more vigorously.

In particular, when implementing improvements, people's understanding and conviction will come more easily if you first point out examples of waste in everyday activities and then stress the need to observe work in the plant with a keen eye.

What I would like to see, then, is a concerted effort made to explain things inductively.

The 90 Percent Strategy

I had not seen Mr. Tsuji of F Electronics for a long while when he told me this story.

"I was so impressed after taking your Production Technology Seminar that I have devoted myself to plant improvement ever since.

When my department head gave me a topic, I carried out on-site surveys and considered the problem from all angles. I'd put together a report outlining what I thought was a perfect improvement plan and take it to the department head's office. He'd glanced through the report and say, 'Tsuji, this won't do. Think it over again and come up with something else.'

" 'But what's wrong with it?' I'd ask.

" 'The whole thing is wrong,' he'd reply. 'Just give it some more thought, all right?'

"I would rethink my proposal and submit it again, but once more I would be sent back to do more work on it. Finally, the third time he would give the plan his approval.

"This sort of thing happened two or three times and I was on the verge of a nervous breakdown. I couldn't get any work done because all I could think about was how incompetent I was and how I wasn't qualified to be a production engineer.

"Around this time, one of the old hands, a section chief named Ueno, noticed that I seemed to be having a hard time of it. 'How about coming over to my place tonight?' he suggested.

"That night, although I wasn't too enthusiastic, I visited Mr. Ueno at home. He gave me a serious talking to and let me in on some secrets. When I went back home I still wasn't sure whether I should believe what he told me or not.

"The next time I got a new topic from my department head, I kept in mind what Mr. Ueno had told me as I drew up and submitted my report. The department head looked at the report and pointed out some things I had left out. And he was right — I had skipped a few things. I apologized and promised to make corrections immediately.

"When I had made the necessary additions and resubmitted the report, the department head chided me for leaving out such elementary things. 'Be more careful from now on,' he said, and then he approved the report by affixing his personal stamp.

"Mr. Ueno told me I'd been unwise to provide my superiors with 100 percent of the answers to the problem. 'Give them 90 percent of the answers and let them hold on to some dignity.' Perhaps I had doubted Mr. Ueno, but when I put his plan into effect I did things a little better than I had been told to.

"The big lesson I learned in all this is that obstinately sticking to your arguments doesn't get you anywhere. You've got to pay attention to human psychology."

Of course not all department heads are like Mr. Tsuji's, but his story reminded me that on occasion one has to think about satisfying the boss's pride.

Improvement Assassins

Nowadays, nearly all Japanese companies have adopted suggestion systems, and many suggestions for improvements are being generated.

Proposals for improvement that come out of the shop must be evaluated. Some evaluators, however, spend most of their time pointing out shortcomings in the proposals they see. They go over one proposal after another and reject them, saying "No good....No good....We've seen this before." I call committee members of this sort *improvement assassins*. People in the shop will rapidly lose interest in making suggestions if their proposals are killed off so readily. They will either start to think all their suggestions are bad ones or question their own abilities, and eventually they will stop making any suggestions at all.

Generally speaking, although the impact of actual proposals received is important, even more crucial is a sense of participation in the company — a sense that everyone wants to work to make his or her own company better. Shop workers' desire to make suggestions will cool in companies with negative-thinking improvement assassins, and only a few diehard "suggestion freaks" will continue to make proposals.

When a proposal is rejected at A Electric, the person who made the suggestion is summoned and the evaluation committee explains to him or her what aspect of the suggestion was unacceptable and why it was not adopted. Then the person who made the proposal is urged to rethink the suggestion. Alternatively, the committee might explain that the suggestion was a good one, but that it could not be adopted because similar proposals had already been submitted. "Keep the good suggestions coming!" the committee urges.

In the past, people in the shop had no way of knowing that similar proposals had already been made and therefore felt dissatisfied because they did not understand why their good ideas had not been adopted. This problem reportedly has disappeared now that the evaluation committee explains the reasons for rejected proposals.

Often, companies kill suggestion activities entirely by presenting awards for prizewinning suggestions but ignoring rejected proposals. We look forward to seeing this issue addressed by the adoption of a system of explaining rejections such as the one used by A Electric.

IE, You E, Everybody E

I first instituted a five day IE improvement course at A Electric in 1962. I made the following remarks at a discussion session on the evening before the final day of the course:

"During the last four days, you have been studying basic IE concepts and techniques, but when you go back to your plants to make improvements, you've got to take back more than just IE. There's one other important thing I want you to remember to take back with you — You E.

"No matter how good you may think your plans are, you must see to it that the people involved understand and are convinced by those plans so they will go out of their way to implement them; they must believe your methods are good ones — that they will generate good products easily.

"So, I want you to remember to take You E back with you along with IE."

At that point, the Manufacturing Department head, Mr. Horii, suggested the problem be tackled in a spirit of "IE, You E, Everybody E." That phrase later became a watchword at A Electric, and improvements progressed smoothly and with lively acceptance in the shop.

Division of Labor Is Not Necessarily a Good Thing

This example involves an operation in which ink is applied over the stamped portion of a golf ball and then, after drying, the surface is wiped off to bring out the imprinted characters.

Workers A and B:

- Take roughly 50 balls apiece and paint ink onto their surfaces with brushes.
- Arrange the balls in no particular order on a workbench.

- After a specified period of time elapses, reveal inked-in characters by wiping with a rag the surfaces of balls that were judged to have dried.

These procedures had shortcomings, however:

- Workers had to determine which balls had dried.
- When workers picked up inadequately dried balls they often smeared the ink.

These shortcomings were overcome in improved procedures that involved a division of labor:

- Worker A painted ink onto the surface of the balls and placed them one by one into a chute provided between worker A and worker B.
- B took the balls in the order they came down the chute and wiped them off.

This method included several innovations:

- There was no need to pick out balls on which ink had dried because adequately dried balls were fed to worker B in order.
- No balls were smeared because none were picked up until fully dry.
- A division of labor eliminated the wasteful operations of picking up and putting down brushes and rags.

The results, however, were mixed:

- The output of imprinted balls rose by roughly 15 percent.
- At the same time, the inking operation was often done crudely, so that inadequately inked characters showed up more frequently. This in turn necessitated increased re-inking operations.
- This lowered the efficiency of imprinting operations by 5 percent.

Overall, then, the operation ended up being cruder because it did not give workers ultimate responsibility for quality.

In the end, the operation was improved as follows:

- Workers A and N each perform the same operations.
- They paint ink onto the surfaces of golf balls.
- Each worker places balls in order onto a turntable that holds

fifty balls. A place is provided for a fifty-first ball, and when only this last space remains, the inking operation is halted.

- Workers use rags to wipe balls on which ink has dried.

This change led to an eventual 10 percent increase in efficiency.

This example underscores the fact that beyond the simplistic view that division of labor increases efficiency, a crucial factor must be considered: people need to take responsibility for their own work.

10

The Force of Habit

ENOUGH IMPROVEMENT PLANS, ALREADY!

According to the physical law of inertia, a body in motion tends to remain in motion and a body at rest tends to remain at rest. In the same way, when human beings perform a given task, they tend to resist any change in the procedures they use.

In this connection, a scientist once performed an experiment to see whether goldfish could remember things. First he built a glass tank with a glass barrier in the middle (see Figure 8); in the center of the barrier he made a hole large enough for a goldfish to swim through.

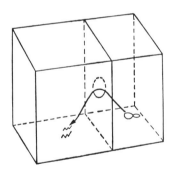

FIGURE 8. Glass Tank

When he placed a goldfish on one side of the barrier and food on the other side, the goldfish headed straight for the food and ran into the transparent pane of glass. After repeating this action a number of times, the goldfish managed to pass through the central hole to the food.

After numerous repetitions, the goldfish would head straight through the hole and eat the food. Apparently, repetition taught the goldfish to remember that all it had to do was swim through the central passage.

Next, the researcher removed the glass barrier and placed the trained goldfish on one side of the tank and food on the other side. In spite of the fact that the barrier was gone, the goldfish still swam to the food via the place where the hole had been. In other words, *force of habit* led the goldfish to persist in its old behavior despite a change in the situation.

Surely, humans too, are affected by the force of habit.

Let me describe another experiment:

An ape was placed inside a cage and given food through bars at the front of the cage (see Figure 9).

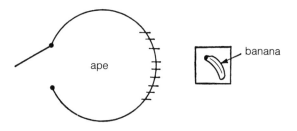

FIGURE 9. Ape Experiment

This method of feeding the ape was repeated over a fairly long period, and the ape eventually became used to finding food when it reached through the bars of the cage. At this point, the food was moved a little farther from the cage, to a spot just out of the ape's reach; then, a door at the back of the cage was left open. Of course, the ape tried to get the food by reaching out through the bars and made repeated attempts to stretch its arm far enough. Eventually, the ape shook the bars in anger.

After a while, the ape noticed that it could go out the back of the cage and circle around to the food.

When the same sort of experiment was carried out with a dog, the dog immediately found the door open, circled around, and took the food. The experiment was also carried out with a five-year-old girl and although she did not circle around as quickly as the dog, she did go through the door more quickly than the ape.

When the same basic experiment was performed with a chicken, the chicken never went out through the door, but merely flapped its wings and crowed.

When a person is presented with a plan for improvement, he will claim that the old way of doing things is easier and want to keep doing things that way. "Enough improvement plans, already," he will say, crowing like a chicken.

I often observe that the force of habit offers powerful resistance to the implementation of plans for improvement.

ARE OLD WAYS BETTER?

It is clearly true that the easiest methods are those we are familiar with. When a method is familiar, we move naturally, without having to think about what should be done next or how each task should be done. Consequently, the job can be carried out without burdening the brain.

This means that there is no psychological burden involved, and a worker can hum as he works. Workers end up believing that familiar operations are the easiest and therefore the best way of doing things.

But is this in fact so?

Lillian M. Gilbreth devised some "tabletop improvement experiments" that help clarify this point.

Experiment 1: Habit

- Write *production engineering* on 15 cards.
- Measure how much time it takes to write each card and graph the values onto a curve, as shown in Figure 10.
- In the language of psychology, your unburdened brain "anticipates" as you write. When you are writing the p, your mind is already telling you to write r next and how to write it. This allows your hand to move fluidly.
- As a result, the task requires very little time and there is minimal deviation among the values obtained. The effect of practice makes itself felt, as well, so times are slightly shorter at the end.

- This familiar method involves only a slight mental burden and little time. The output of letters — i.e., quality — is stable.

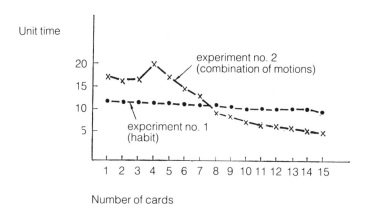

Unit time

Number of cards

FIGURE 10. Time per Card in Seconds

Experiment 2: Combined Motions

- Write the first letter of *production engineering* but not the second letter. Then write the third letter but not the fourth. Continue writing every other letter. Repeat this process fifteen times.
- The correct outcome will be *p o u t o e g n e i g*.

Figure 10 gives the results of this experiment. Even though you wrote only half as many letters as in Experiment 1, writing the letters the first four times took far more than half the time needed for the first four repetitions in the first experiment. The fourth and fifth repetitions took a particularly long time. Increasingly less time was needed after that, so that the fifteenth writing took far less time than in Experiment 1.

Discussion

Why did writing letters in Experiment 2 take more time at first than writing the letters in Experiment 1 even though only half as many letter were involved?

The answer is that, in Experiment 2, after writing *p* you had to think about what letter to write next. You had to determine that the next letter was *o* and the one after that was *t*, etc. Thinking as you wrote each letter entailed hesitation and the process took more time because the next letter was not automatically anticipated.

As you wrote out the letters in Experiment 2 several times, however, an image of the sequence, *p o u t o*, etc. began to form and writing grew more fluid as mental anticipation began to occur. At this point, the fact that you were writing fewer letters began to take effect and total time diminished.

The fourth and fifth repetitions took so much time because time was taken up verifying that the letters were indeed the correct ones. This is a normal response that ordinarily occurs when people are faced with a new task.

Thus, even though there is no question that dealing with half the number of letters is an improvement, initial decisions and hesitations will keep mental anticipation from taking over and will entail considerable difficulty and time. In addition, quality may occasionally suffer as you write the wrong letters.

As you write the sequence over and over again, however, you will gradually memorize the new task and mental anticipation will occur. You will end up learning *p o u t o e g n e i g* as a single phrase and decision and hesitation will vanish, allowing the effect of fewer letters to take over. In the end, then, it will take less time than Experiment 1.

Since improvements to a greater or lesser extent demand new procedures, a certain amount of difficulty will be encountered and a certain amount of time will be needed to decide how to carry out those new procedures and then to memorize them. Initially, then, new methods will be difficult. Old procedures, however, are easy just because they are familiar; just as mental anticipation made it easy to write the larger number of letters smoothly.

This explanation is no doubt accurate, but is it really reasonable to go on to claim that old ways are easier *and therefore better*? For instance, as long as it is unfamiliar, even an improved procedure will be more difficult and will take more time than the old procedure because decisions and hesitations will occur and because mental anticipation is absent. Thus, no improvement shows its true worth right away. Its real efficacy will become apparent only after a certain period of practice.

This means that 99 percent of all improvement plans would vanish without a trace if they were to be abandoned after only a brief trial. People in charge of plant improvement must grasp this fact, so that they can provide necessary encouragement when people on the shop floor complain during trial implementation that the improved procedures are too hard or take too long. "Keep at it a little bit longer," they have to say. "Improvements are nearly always more difficult at first."

If shop workers say that the supposedly improved procedures take just as much time as the old methods, the response must be, "That's only true because you aren't accustomed to them yet. Once you get used to the new procedures, they will definitely take less time." Once again, people must be given strong encouragement and urged to continue with the improved procedures.

In a surprising number of cases, however, supervisors will agree with workers that new methods take too long or are too difficult and will abandon them right away. It is crucial to recognize that this attitude is entirely wrong.

In any event, while it is absolutely true that old ways are easier, it is a mistake to conclude that they are therefore better. It is important to understand that even the finest improvements will not demonstrate their true worth until they have become familiar.

DOWN WITH GOOD FORM!

Improvement work by people at M Electric in Himeji had reportedly resulted in the reduction of two-hour press setups to about 12 minutes. I was invited to the plant to observe the outcome of this work and to give advice regarding any further areas needing improvement.

I went to the plant and before I went into the shop I asked the people from the company to explain what specific improvements they had made and what procedures were followed in the setups. At that point, I pointed out further possible improvements, and when these were put into effect, setup time dropped to 8 minutes and 27 seconds.

We then went to an auditorium where I addressed a gathering of some 150 M Electric engineers and executives from affiliated firms on the basic SMED concepts and techniques for SMED implementation. At the end of my talk, I told a story.

"You are familiar with the expression, 'good form.' As you know, some people with poor handicaps still talk a good game of golf and have a fine swing — indeed, they look like pros. 'Good form' types are people who, when they actually get out on the course and play, don't quite keep up with their own tales and end up hitting over 100. In other words, they're fine as long as they don't hit the ball, but they're no good when they do. Talking by itself doesn't raise your score.

"I used to work in Taiwan, and for about ten years I served as an advisor to Taiwanese companies. During those ten years, I became good friends with a Mr. Ts'ai, a director of Taiwan Plastics. Whenever I visited Taiwan, I went to the Hsintanshui Golf Course for an early morning game of golf with Mr. and Mrs. Ts'ai. We made it a point to start at 6 o'clock, play one round by 8 A.M. and get to the company by 9 A.M. Mr. Ts'ai's handicap was about 12, so I didn't win much, but Mrs. Ts'ai's handicap of 29 meant that on a good day I might win. This only happened about one game in ten. Mrs. Ts'ai usually hit the ball farther than I could. Not wanting to be outdone, I'd hit the ball with all my might, but it usually fell far short of Mrs. Ts'ai's ball.

"One day after Mrs. Ts'ai had beaten me rather thoroughly, I was reluctantly eating a bowlful of Taiwanese noodles when Mr. Ts'ai came up and spoke to me.

"'You may be getting on in years, Dr. Shingo, but you certainly do swing at the ball with everything you've got. In the game of golf, though, it doesn't matter how hard you swing — the ball isn't going anywhere unless your club makes contact.' That remark woke me up. Just as Mr. Ts'ai had said, I had been concentrating on a big, strong swing, and I'd ended up either clipping the top or cutting under the bottom of the ball. The club wasn't striking the ball square on. 'In golf,' I reflected, 'you've got to hit the ball correctly.'

"After I returned to Japan the following day, I was invited to a party given by M Metals at a Hachiōji golf course. When we got down to playing, I gave up the idea of slamming the ball and paid attention to bringing the club in contact with the ball. As a result, I got 51 out, 49 in and, with a first-time score of 100, I ended up in third place.

" 'There's no question about it,' I said to myself, 'no matter how good you may sound when you talk about golf, you're not going to get any better if you don't hit the ball.' By the same token, with SMED, actually trying out ideas is crucial, rather than thinking up reasons why ideas might not work. 'The proper form,' I concluded, 'is never going to lead to any results.' "

In the audience, Mr. Miyauchi of Fukushin Electric found that this story appealed to him. He told me that his own handicap was 12, so what I had to say really hit home.

Mr. Miyauchi returned to his company the following day and called company executives together. "Starting right now," he announced, "we're going to adopt the SMED system." Sure enough, people came up with one reason after another why the innovation would not work. "No way," said one person. "It's impossible to cut hour-long setups down to nine minutes or less." Someone else protested that, "SMED will cost too much because it requires standardizing all the dies."

"Don't let me hear about how things *ought* to be done!" Mr. Miyauchi thundered in a resounding rejection of such protests. He took the lead right away and by concentrating on improvements (such as die height standardization, one-touch centering, and standardization of clamping surfaces) for only two dies, they were able to make a trial run of new procedures in the afternoon of that same day — a trial in which they were able to cut a 1 hour and 20-minute press setup to a mere 7 minutes and 24 seconds. The executives who observed this feat were astonished and success gave everyone a surge of confidence. Changed attitudes and dedicated efforts toward improvement resulted in the superb achievement of bringing simultaneous setups on six 70-ton presses down to the six-minute level with a team of three men and three women.

From that point on, the rate of improvement in the company increased visibly. Whenever people come up with reasons why a new method will not work, they are told not to pay attention to *form*, or to how things *ought* to be done; they find some way to work through any problems that arise.

CAN YOU EVER BE TOO BUSY FOR IMPROVEMENT?

Frequently, when I go to production plants and promote improvement, I am rebuffed by people who say they are too busy and have no time for such activities. If business has slowed down a bit the next time I visit and I suggest that perhaps now there is time for improvement, I am often turned down outright. "We've got no work to do," people will say. "We're busy looking for work and haven't got any time. Anyway, it's hard to get fired up about improvement when there's no work — no need to, either."

At this rate, there's no telling when improvements can be made. I make it a point to respond by telling people, "Look, you'll stop being busy either when you die or when the company goes bankrupt. Think about it. It's precisely because you are busy that you've got to analyze the factors that keep you busy. Revitalize the company by changing those factors for the better."

No salaried worker will ever save money if he or she decides to put away only what's left over at the end of the month. If you want to save, you've got to decide to have a fixed payroll deduction and then live on the rest. You'll never be able to own your own home unless you use that accumulated savings as a down payment and then pay monthly installments.

I have built three houses in my lifetime; the first was when I was a 27-year-old bachelor. Why wait until you retire so you can use your retirement money to build a house?

The same thing holds for improvement. No company can develop unless efforts at improvement are sustained with the regularity of payroll deductions — through good times and bad, whether busy or not. It seems to me that a company that refuses to sustain improvement work is past the stage of needing a doctor. It's going to have to be taken to a priest and then to the cemetery.

I visited Yoshioka Plating when the worldwide economy was in such bad shape during the oil crisis. Construction work was under way there on new automated plating equipment. I asked the company's president why they had begun such costly construction when business was so bad.

"Actually," he replied. "It was my father's last wish."

"What do you mean by that?"

"My father," the president said, "always told me that I would make a lot of money if I kept plant facilities running hard when I was busy. He taught me that I should use slack periods to rebuild and augment equipment. For one thing, if you invest in facilities during slumps, big equipment makers who wouldn't even look at you when they're busy will figure that you're running a solid operation. They'll be receptive to unusual specifications and other requests, and you can have things done at relatively low cost. What's more, there will be no negative impact if you have to halt plant operations for a while."

I marveled at the wisdom of the father who had left such a legacy and at the son who had the courage to put it into effect.

THE "DYNAMITE HOLE" APPROACH TO IMPROVEMENT

It goes without saying that to improve work in production plants requires that everyone in the workplace understand the improvements, be persuaded by them, and actively work to put them into effect. In the early stages of improvement, however, it can be effective to use a "dynamite hole" approach.

When cutting a tunnel for extracting ore from a mine, rather than working the entire tunnel face with a mandrel, it is more efficient to drill holes with a small bit, pack the holes with dynamite, attach a fuse, and throw a switch — the electric current will blast open the tunnel.

Given the difficulty of getting everybody to think the same way, you should choose active people — vigorous department or section heads and, in particular, shop floor foremen and group leaders — and persuade them first. By way of experiment, have them first focus on a single topic and demonstrate their success to everyone else. This initial topic need not involve the most crucial task in the plant, but making it visible is the quickest route to persuading everyone that improvement really is possible.

People in the shop simply will not be convinced if all you do is give them logical arguments.

If you have as many as 100 people in a group, it is difficult to get them all headed in the same direction. Generally, one third of the people in a given group will be in favor of a new proposal, one third will be against it, and the remaining third will be neutral. By bringing even one person from among the neutral third over to your way of thinking, you can bring the neutral faction surging over to the "yea" side to form an absolute majority. When this happens, the remaining "nays" will naturally come around as well.

Look at it another way. If you start by aiming for 70 percent success rather than 100 percent, successful implementation of a new scheme will get everyone to believe in it and the climate in the entire workplace can be shifted in the direction of improvement.

When I want to implement SMED, I have workers bring out two dies for machines of approximately 100 tons or less. In the course of about an hour, I carry out a demonstration:

- Use blocks to make die heights uniform.
- Secure blocks at clamping sites with gummed tape and use clamps.
- Place blocks on the far sides of dies so that the dies are centered when they strike the stoppers.
- Bring a new die near the machine during external setup.
- If possible, have two workers carry out parallel operations.
- Keep all needed tools within reach.

Without exception, these procedures make it possible right away to reduce setups of an hour and a half to seven or eight minutes.

Seeing a demonstration like this helps people see that SMED is possible, and improvement is frequently speeded up because categorical opposition to SMED vanishes.

The first time I visited the French auto maker Citroën, in 1981, I spent the first morning talking about production control to about 50 management people and engineers. I had a hard time getting on with my speech, because objections kept popping up while I was lecturing. In particular, a welter of objections came up when I talked about SMED. "It can't be done," said some. Others said, "It'll be too expensive," or "You'll need incredibly expensive equipment."

When operations began that afternoon, I went to the plant and had two dies brought out. I checked their dimensions myself and then asked to have some needed work done. I said that I wanted blocks of such and such size in certain places and 50 mm² blocks in other places to make clamping surfaces uniform.

In my lecture that afternoon, continual questions and objections arose, just as they had in the morning.

When we went to observe the SMED demonstration the following morning, what had been a 1 hour and 40-minute setup had been shortened to a mere 12 minutes. The engineers and the management people looking on were stunned.

We returned to the conference room afterwards and I gave everyone a little talk.

"Before I left Japan, I was told that the French were very argumentative and my experience yesterday confirms that appraisal. It seems to me, however, that all your arguments were negative ones, such as 'This won't work' or 'That's impossible.'

"As I see it, no matter how informed your opinions are, you'll never make any progress if you insist that things are impossible. In Japan, when arguments are deadlocked, we still believe new methods to be possible. We give them a try and look at actual results to find ways of overcoming problems. I am persuaded that this is the most important reason for Japan's having raised the level of her industry and succeeded in producing high-quality, inexpensive products.

"Instead of sitting around conference tables and trading arguments whenever doubts arise, how about actually giving new ideas a try and seeing what happens?"

This time no one objected, because they had all seen the success of SMED in action.

From that point on, not only did the people at Citroen listen to what I had to say, but their positive efforts brought significant success. SMED was achieved on most machines and inventories were slashed by more than half.

Indeed, we might draw an analogy between this simple two-die SMED demonstration and drilling holes for dynamite.

NEVER SAY "IMPOSSIBLE"

One day I had lunch with Mr. Kōno, a director of Z Machinery. What he told me that day was of some interest:

"Mr. M, the president of our parent company, M Diesel, succeeded in producing the first Japanese diesel engines. He's a dedicated entrepreneur who tenaciously devotes himself to getting the job done.

"One morning he showed up at the Engineering Department and said he had thought up a new design for an engine. 'I want a prototype built and tested before the end of tomorrow,' he said. 'Who will do it for me?' The engineers all hung their heads in silence, each fearing that he might be chosen. 'Do a four-week job in two days?' they asked themselves. 'Impossible!'

"Seeing their reaction, the president continued calmly: 'Well, it seems there are no volunteers. I suppose I'll just have to do it myself.'

"Mr. M then flopped down in a chair next to a young engineer and began giving him instructions on how to draw up plans for the engine. He telephoned an old fellow who had long done work for him and, as soon as the first page of plans was completed, he had the old man take it by bicycle over to a wooden pattern workshop. One by one, he gave directions for the building of wooden mock-up parts for the engine. When complete plans had been drawn up, Mr. M went to the workshop himself, sat next to a woodworker, and had the mock-up finished according to his instructions. As soon as each piece of the wooden mock-up was finished, Mr. M had it taken back to his own company's casting shop and had a casting die made. Soon it began to look as though the casting dies would be finished that night, so he had the foreman in charge of melting show up early the following morning and had each piece cast. As each piece was completed, it was taken to the machine shop and finished. Here, too, Mr. M sat next to the machine and gave step-by-step instructions. By the end of the following day, the engine had taken shape and trials could be run in overtime."

Mr. Kōno had said that building the engine in two days was impossible and he had bet a cake that it couldn't be done. When the testing was completed, the president turned to Mr. Kōno and said, "Well, how about it?" So Mr. Kōno had a cake purchased and served it to everyone involved.

Mr. Kōno had watched the company president in action throughout the task and he was powerfully impressed. "If you are really dedicated and determined to accomplish something," he told me, "it doesn't matter if others think it's impossible — you can do it. All right, then, I vowed to myself: As long as I live, I swear I will never again say anything is impossible."

Two months afterward, the president of the company again came to work early. "This time," he said, "I've thought of a new transmission. Who will make one for me before the end of the day to-

morrow?" The other engineers said nothing, but Mr. Kōno coura-
geously offered to get the job done somehow. Working in much the
same way the president had, Mr. Kōno completed the task by the
close of the following day. Under normal circumstances, the work
would have taken three weeks to carry out.

This success increased Mr. Kōno's confidence and he vowed
again that he would never use the word "impossible" as long as he
lived. Mr. Kōno concluded his story by telling me that, since then, he
has not once said that anything was "impossible." As I listened to Mr.
Kōno's story, I felt deep admiration for the dedication and tenacity of
the founder of Z Machinery.

A PROBLEM WITH THE MIRACLE DRUG?

When I began visiting companies and production plants, there
was one thing I almost always used to tell company presidents: "The
medicine I am prescribing for you is a miracle drug and very powerful, but there is one problem with it."

"What problem?" they would say.

"The problem," I would explain, "is that the medicine won't
work unless you take it. I may tell you wonderful things, but you're
not going to be successful unless you actually do what I'm telling
you. There are a lot of people in this world who worry that medicine
might be bitter or might have side effects, and who find excuses to
avoid swallowing it. Behavior like that will never lead to success. Are
you ready to take your medicine?"

"Sure," the executives always tell me. "We'll make it a point to
take it."

Afterword

THE JAPAN MANAGEMENT ASSOCIATION YEARS

Various recollections come back to me as I review the more than 50 years I have spent working for plant improvement. The first work I did as a professional was an improvement survey at the railway car manufacturing facilities of Hitachi Limited's Kasado plant. In the course of the survey, I was charged with analyzing a process involving pins for connecting rods. Pins had to be transported from the forge to the vicinity of machines in the machining plant, yet a crane busy with other operations sometimes delayed this procedure for about half an hour. Should these periods of time be designated "delays" or "time waiting for crane"? If they were delays, were they process delays or temporary delays? I found myself unable to respond when these questions were put to me.

Until that point, I had always been taught that what resulted from a large-unit analysis of production activities was a process analysis and what came out of a small-unit analysis was an operations analysis. Long delays were process delays and short delays were temporary delays.

Unable to decide how to characterize the thirty minutes or so when pins waited for the crane, I consulted with people from the Japan Management Association who accompanied us, but opinion was divided and no conclusion was reached. After long thought that night, the answer finally dawned on me.

That's it! Process analysis is an analysis of the process by which raw materials are transformed into finished products, and an operations analysis is an analysis of the work which human beings or machines perform on items. I understood that production activities formed a *network of processes and operations*, and that the two

161

phenomena should not be distinguished by the size of units of analysis. Thus, when production is being carried out through lot operations, a *process delay* occurs when items sent to a process wait until processing of the previous lot is completed. Similarly, a *lot delay* occurs when, while one item in a lot is being processed, the remaining items wait — either as unfinished goods or as finished goods. The two kinds of delays must be distinguished, not by the length of time they take, but by their inherent characteristics.

I realized for the first time that process delays begin to disappear only when processes are synchronized and lot delays cannot be resolved unless processing, inspection, and transport lot sizes equal one. For me, this insight was fundamental in subsequent clarification and improvement of production activities.

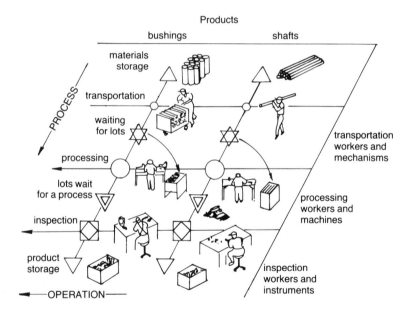

Fɪɢᴜʀᴇ 11. The Structure of Production

This insight helped me understand the significance of Frank Gilbreth's assertion that a process can be broken down into four phenomena: processing, inspection, transportation, and delays. It also helped me explain, in a concise and logical manner, how processing operations, inspection operations, transport operations and delay operations correspond to each of these four phenomena. This fact had considerable impact on subsequent production activity improvements.

During this same period, I improved the layout of machines at a woodworking plant by grouping them according to processes. To accomplish this, I came up with the idea of grouping similar pro-

Operation \ Process	Work	Inspection	Transportation	Storage
Preparation, After Adjustment Operations (Setup Operations)	◎	◇	⌀	△
Principal Operations — Main Operations	◎	◈	⌀	△
Principal Operations — Incidental Operations	○	◇	⌀	△
Margin Allowances — Fatigue Allowances	○	◇	⌀	△
Margin Allowances — Hygiene Allowances	○	◇	⌀	△
Margin Allowances — Operations Allowances	○	◇	⌀	△
Margin Allowances — Workplace Allowances	○	◇	⌀	△

FIGURE 12. **The Relationship Between Processes and Operations**

cesses on the basis of noninterference values. This approach I explained later on in *Techniques for Improving Machine Layout* (in Japanese), 1965.

* * * * * * *

In 1948 I served as a lecturer's assistant at the 40-day third Production Technology Course sponsored by the Japan Management Association at Hitachi, Ltd.'s Fujita plant. When A, a course participant sent by a locomotive company, submitted his answer to a machine layout problem assigned by a course instructor, he was told that his solution wouldn't work.

"What's wrong with it?" he countered.

"Long years of experience tell me it won't work," the instructor replied.

But A refused to give up. "I can't accept that sort of explanation," he said.

As I sat to one side listening, I asked myself why a dispute like this was occurring. I wondered why it wasn't possible to make clearer judgments about the relative merits of layouts. I later realized that the point of a layout scheme is to minimize transport. Making transport more rational is a very different issue from making *transport operations* more rational. I developed a method for determining machine layout via what I call coefficients of ease of transport, and in 1951 the concept was applied to the layout of the Furukawa Electric Company's copper rolling mill at Nikkō. I later systematized these methods in my 1965 book *Techniques for Improving Machine Layout*.

I had bid farewell to the primitive method of determining the relative merits of layouts by using simple flow charts.

* * * * * * *

For three years, from 1956 to 1958, I was stationed at Mitsubishi Heavy Industries' Nagasaki shipyards as the head of an improvement survey team. By the end of 1956, we had developed a new production method and achieved a world's record by reducing the four months usually required to construct the hull of a 65,000-ton ship (in this case the *World Independence*) and shortening it to three months. Our methods spread to other Japanese ship manufacturers and contributed significantly to keeping Japan in the forefront of the shipbuilding industry worldwide.

As this three-year project came to a close I left the Japan Management Association and founded the Institute for Management Improvement, where I began to blaze new trails as an improvement consultant.

THE INSTITUTE FOR MANAGEMENT IMPROVEMENT YEARS

In 1950, I conducted a survey at Mazda KK in Hiroshima — at the time Tōyō Industries. It was a week-long work analysis aimed at solving the problem of insufficient capacity on an 800-ton press. I was shocked to observe how press operations were curtailed when, in the midst of a tooling setup, the discovery of a missing bolt sent workers on a long search. This episode revealed to me the most fundamental idea behind the SMED concept, that a setup consists of two essential elements: *internal setup*, which must be performed while a machine is off, and *external setup*, which can be carried out while the machine is operating.

On a visit to Mitsubishi Heavy Industries's Hiroshima shipyards in 1957, plant manager Matsuzō Okazaki and I achieved dramatic success when we came up with a remarkable new method for improved operations.

To increase the capacity of a large open-sided planer used for machining diesel engine beds, we took the strikingly inefficient procedure of centering and dimensioning on the planer table while the machine was turned off, and constructed a second planer table, so that centering and dimensioning could be done on the second table while the planer was running. Capacity could be improved substantially simply by switching tables.

This achievement foreshadowed the development of the second key idea that made SMED possible — shifting internal setup to external setup.

The final encounter leading to SMED took place during an improvement survey at Toyota Motor Corporation in 1969. Setup changes on a 1,000-ton press at Toyota were taking four hours, while in Germany, Volkswagen was performing the setups in two hours. The Toyota plant manager, Taiichi Ohno, had given instructions to overtake the Germans. Over the course of six months, we clearly separated internal setup from external setup, and then improved all the operations involved in each, with the result that we succeeded in cutting setup time to one and a half hours.

When I visited the plant the following month, I found that new instructions had been issued, this time to cut setup times to three minutes. My first thought was that the task was simply impossible. After all, it had taken us half a year to get the time down to an hour and a half. But then I had a flash of inspiration.

It occurred to me that at the Mitsubishi shipyards in Hiroshima we had in fact shifted internal setup to external setup. At once, I jotted out eight principles for shortening setup times on the nearest blackboard. Thanks to the outstanding efforts of Mr. Ikebuchi, the supervisor in charge, and Mr. Ohno, the foreman, we were able to get the setup down to three minutes within three months. With the hope that any setup change could be carried out in less than ten minutes, I dubbed our method the SMED System, for "Single [-digit] Minute Exchange of Die." This SMED system was incorporated into — and became one of the pivotal techniques of — the Toyota Production System. SMED was applied in a broad range of industries throughout Japan and went on to contribute significantly to a revolution in production methods.

The SMED system was subsequently introduced in Europe and the United States and reaped tremendous success as it spread throughout the world.

Taiichi Ohno's demand that a setup that had already been shortened from four hours to an hour and a half be further cut to three minutes sounded preposterous; but it was that demand that occasioned the birth of SMED. As far as I am concerned, SMED might never have seen the light of day had it not been for those few words from Mr. Ohno. For this reason, Mr. Ohno's is a name I will never forget as long as I live. As I have done on previous occasions, I would like to express my thanks to him.

* * * * * * *

In 1951, when I was head of the Education Division of the Japan Management Institute, a Mr. Y from Nippon Electric came to see me at my office one day.

"Do you know about quality control?" he asked me.

"You mean carrying out strict inspections to reduce defects?" I replied.

"Wrong," Mr. Y replied. "It's not quality control if you don't use statistics."

For more than two hours he explained the use of statistics in sampling inspections, use of control charts in quality control methods, use of statistics in experimental planning methods, determination of significant differences, and so forth.

"From now on," he emphasized, "you can't have quality control unless you rely on the scientific, logical methods of statistics." Fully persuaded, I set out to study statistical quality control (SQC) methods at the Japan Management Association and I put those methods to considerable use in the course of plant surveys.

I was taught that informative inspection was basic to a statistical quality control system. Defects would decrease, I was told, if feedback was given and corrective action taken in response to any abnormality, i.e., any situation in which control limits were exceeded. The so-called judgment inspection used in the past performs only a passive function, examining finished goods and distinguishing between acceptable and defective items to keep defects from being passed on to customers. The ability to actually *reduce* defects is totally lacking in judgment inspection. I firmly believed, however, that informative inspection provided a truly innovative and ideal method of quality control. I maintained an especially fervent belief in approaches founded on statistical science.

In 1961, Yamada Electric in Nagoya told me that they were having trouble with workers' forgetting to insert springs in switch assemblies, and I went to the plant to observe the situation.

The operation was extremely simple. The task consisted of inserting small springs inside *on* and *off* buttons in box-shaped switches. As I watched, however, a worker forgot to put in a spring. The department head immediately called out to the worker, warning her to pay closer attention to the job.

At this point, I asked the department head what it meant when humans forget something.

"To forget?" he replied. "It just means — well — to forget, doesn't it?"

"And what do you mean when you say 'to forget means to forget'?" I persisted.

This time there was no reply.

"Listen," I said. "There are two kinds of forgetting. The first involves simply forgetting something. Since people are not perfect, they will, on rare occasions, inadvertently forget things. The other type of forgetting involves forgetting that one has forgotten something. Knowing that we are prone to this type of forgetting prompts us to use checklists. That way, even if we forget something, the checklist will remind us and keep us, in the end, from leaving anything out.

"Why not," I suggested, "incorporate the function of a checklist in this operation?"

Some changes were made:

- In the old method, a worker began by taking two springs out of a large parts box and then assembled a switch.
- In the new approach, a small dish is placed in front of the parts box and the worker's first task is to take two springs out of the box and place them on the dish. Then the worker assembles the switch. If any spring remains on the dish, then the worker knows he or she has forgotten to insert it.

This procedure has eliminated the failure to include springs in switch assemblies. The approach used here applies a foolproofing idea originally developed for safety reasons.

Borrowing this same idea for quality control, when foolproofing mechanisms are installed throughout a process, the results are surprising. Defects either disappear altogether or are nearly eliminated.

Providing a foolproofing device at Arakawa Auto Body to prevent parts from being turned around in a welding operation did away with defects, but brought one of the workers to tears. "Have I really been such a fool?" she asked. She stayed home the following day and the department head went to see her to convince her that no one ever meant to question her intelligence. This episode pointed out to me the unfortunate connotations of the term "foolproofing," so I devised a new name, *poka-yoke*, or "mistake-proofing," to refer to inadvertent mistakes (in Japanese, *poka*) that anyone might make. The expression *poka-yoke* is used in the context of the Toyota Production System and the Japanese word is sometimes used untranslated, even in Europe and the United States.

The fact that widespread use of poka-yoke devices cuts defect rates dramatically, weakened my belief in the SQC approach, for it made me realize that defects can be reduced without relying on SQC.

In 1964, Hayata Tokizane, the managing director of Matsushita Electric's television operations, told me that he didn't want a single

Matsushita television to be defective. "An individual customer," he explained, "only buys one television set. If that one set is defective, then the customer might assume that all Matsushita television sets are lemons. I'm always after my people, telling them that we mustn't make a single defective set no matter how many tens of thousands we produce."

I replied that I thought his attitude seemed reasonable. But then something occurred to me: if the goal is zero defects, why use sampling inspections in plants at all? On the other hand though, if sampling inspection is backed by statistical science there shouldn't be anything wrong with them. As I rode the Shinkansen "bullet" train back to Tokyo, I wrestled with the contradiction between these two arguments.

After grappling with the problem for some time, as the train neared Tokyo, I suddenly figured out the answer. A sampling inspection is nothing more than a rational *method* of inspection; in no way does it make quality assurance itself more rational.

This means that although sampling inspection provides a rational way to make inspection less bothersome, 100 percent inspection is definitely preferable in terms of quality assurance. To put the matter succinctly, 100 percent inspection is thorough but it is also a nuisance. What we need to assure quality is 100 percent inspection that is trouble free. And the most effective way to do that, I concluded, is to use poka-yoke devices.

I did some more thinking. Why, I wondered, do poka-yoke applications produce two types of results — cases in which defects disappear completely, and cases in which defects are vastly reduced but do not vanish altogether? This line of thought led me, in 1967, to the concept of *source inspection*. In some cases, poka-yoke devices perform 100 percent inspection to discover that defects have occurred. In other instances, however, they can detect errors that underlie defects. In those cases, immediate feedback and corrective action can prevent the errors from turning into defects.

In 1971, on my first overseas study tour, I visited the Wotan Company in Frankfurt, West Germany. There, one of my colleagues, Mr. K, asked our hosts if they carried out quality control. "Of course we do," the chief engineer replied.

"And yet," said Mr. K, "you haven't got a single control chart posted in your plant."

"What's a control chart?" the engineer asked.

With a triumphant air, Mr. K proceeded to explain control

charts to the Wotan representative. At length the engineer replied, "That's a very interesting idea, but don't you think it's fundamentally wrong-headed?"

"What are you talking about?" Mr. K retorted.

"In what you've just described, you take action after defects have already occurred. Our approach is to take action before the defects show up in the first place. By the way," the Wotan engineer continued, "what's the defect rate at your company?"

"Only about 2.5 percent," said Mr. K.

"That's interesting," our host replied. "Our defect rate is about 0.3 percent."

At this, Mr. K lapsed into silence.

The Wotan engineer explained that a quality control chief checked tools and bits after they were set in machines and that operations began only after the chief had given his OK.

This, I realized, was a source inspection approach, and the episode deepened my confidence in source inspection.

In 1977, I saw with my own eyes how the Shizuoka plant of Matsushita's Washing Machine Division had succeeded in attaining a continuous record of one month with zero defects on a drainpipe assembly line involving 23 workers. I was finally released from the spell of SQC methods when I saw that their success had been achieved principally through the installation of poka-yoke devices that prevented defects from occurring.

Now I could argue that zero defects could be achieved by using source inspection and the poka-yoke system.

* * * * * * *

When I visited Saga Tekkōsho's Fujisawa plant in 1969, the plant manager, Mr. Yatagai, asked why people still had to stand by machines even though the machines had been automated. "Why, indeed?" I replied. The serious thought I gave to this question resulted in my arriving at the concept of *pre-automation*.

Theorists tell us that total automation is achieved in 23 steps, of which the first 20 involve only mechanization, and not automation at all. Full automation, furthermore, requires a mechanism that can detect abnormal conditions and deal with them on its own. These two requirements — detecting abnormal conditions and taking corrective measures — are difficult to achieve, however, so I use the term pre-automation to refer to the stage just before total automation where the mechanism detects abnormal conditions, but corrective measures are carried out by humans.

Applying this concept to the workplace, some 90 percent of the effects of total automation can be secured for a mere 10 percent or so of the cost of total automation. By running machines without supervision, during lunch breaks and after hours, this approach has been tremendously effective in raising output and in improving productivity.

* * * * * * *

In 1973 I toured West Germany and Switzerland to introduce the SMED system. At a Daimler-Benz plant in West Germany, I was astonished to see die-cast goods on which no burrs whatsoever had been generated. Until then, I had assumed all die casting produced burrs and that the problem lay in finding the best way to remove them. Not in my wildest dreams had I imagined a method of die casting in which no burrs were produced in the first place. I asked how it was that no burrs were generated.

"It's because," I was told, "for ten years we've been using our own low-pressure casting method. It works like this: after the die is secured, we create a vacuum inside and then inject molten aluminum."

"Of course!" I thought. Casting involves exchanging molten liquid for a vacuum. Indeed, it was as though I had forgotten that the earth is surrounded by air.

After this encounter, I visited the Buhler Company, a Swiss manufacturer of the vacuum die-casting machines, and on my return to Japan I worked to persuade people of the effectiveness of vacuum casting. Believing that the notion of vacuum forming could be applied to resin molding as well as to metal die-casting, I put the idea into practice at Daiya Plastics in Osaka in 1975. The results were magnificent, not only in terms of quality improvement and defect reduction, but also with respect to shortened cycle times. Moreover, with vacuum-forming equipment costs of only ¥ 1 million ($3,300), the experiment showed an excellent rate of return on investment.

I have since encouraged other companies to adopt vacuum-forming methods, and although so far only a few firms have put the idea into practice, I am pleased at the splendid results that each of them has achieved.

* * * * * * *

These and other experiences were collected in my 1978 book, *Fundamental Approaches to Plant Improvement* (in Japanese). In that work, I presented my basic philosophy of plant improvement. In particular, I stressed the following methods.

With respect to the process elements:

- *Processing*: Vacuum forming and VE
- *Inspection*: Source inspection and the poka-yoke system
- *Transport*: Improved layout (determining machine placement on the basis of coefficients of ease of transport)
- *Delay*: Drastic reduction of production periods
- *Process delays*: Synchronization and full-work control systems
- *Lot delays*: One-piece flow operations (with improved layout as a prerequisite)

And for operations:

- *Improved preparation and after adjustment*: Single-Minute Exchange of Die, the SMED system
- *Principal operations*: Pre-automation

THE MOVE TO THE INTERNATIONAL ARENA

My basic philosophy is outlined in two works. Improvement concepts are presented in *Systematic Thinking for Plant Improvement* (in Japanese), 1980. Production improvements are collected in *Fundamental Approaches to Plant Improvement* (in Japanese), 1978. Despite the considerable shock sustained by many firms at the beginning of the oil crisis in 1973 – 1974, the unfalteringly excellent performance of the Toyota Motor Corporation focused widespread attention on the Toyota Production System. One after another, scholars and journalists came out with books claiming to reveal the "secrets" of the Toyota Production System. I found these works to be so full of errors and misapprehensions that I feared the true nature of the system would never reach a wide audience.

Since 1955, through my production seminars and consulting work, I had seen the Toyota Production System take shape and develop firsthand, and I firmly believed that both my convictions about what a production system should be and the application of the

SMED approach were having a tremendous impact on that system. I kept silent, however, because of the powerful taboo against a consultant's revealing anything about companies with which he has been involved. Misconceptions about the system continued to abound, however, and I was especially alarmed by people who took the *kanban* method to be the pivotal element in the system — people who thought that the Toyota Production System and kanban were synonymous.

In 1978, Taiichi Ohno, then the central figure in the Toyota Production System, published a book entitled, *The Toyota Production System* (English version forthcoming, Productivity Press, fall 1987). As a specialist in production engineering, I then ventured to write *The Toyota Production System — An Industrial Engineering Study* (in Japanese), in 1980, based on Mr. Ohno's and other published works. This book explained the concepts behind the Toyota Production System and presented specific techniques for putting those concepts into practice. The work struck a responsive chord with many production managers and production engineers and, in 1981, led to a consulting trip to Citroën Automobile Company in France — the first consulting work I had done for an overseas firm.

Still, the overwhelming perception — or misperception — abroad was that the Toyota Production System was a kanban system. People affiliated with Toyota even discussed the kanban system on television in New York. At international managers' conferences it was usually the kanban system that was the focus of discussion.

Hearing all this made me worry that knowledge about the Toyota Production System was being distorted in transmission to foreign countries, and I decided to use my own funds to release an English translation of my own study of the Toyota Production System. This was published in November of 1981 as *Study of Toyota Production System from Industrial Engineering Viewpoint*.

Since I had financed its publication myself, I had no proper channels for marketing the book abroad. Around this time, a friend introduced me to Paul Miller, the editor of the American journal *Tooling and Production*. In 1981, Norman Bodek, the president of Productivity, Inc., and Jack Warne, the president of Omark Industries, came to Japan to observe production methods. Greatly impressed by high productivity on a visit to the Nippondensō Company, they asked if any reference books were available and happened to get hold of copies of my book, which, I am told, they read in the plane flying back to the United States. Mr. Warne immediately ordered 500 copies of the book and had his managers study it.

As a result of putting its ideas into practice, Omark cut production periods of 57 days to three days and four-hour setup changes to two and a half minutes. These impressive results were just the beginning. Defects were cut dramatically, productivity improved, and stocks were slashed by as much as 94 percent. Success followed on success with increasing rapidity, and newspapers and magazines introduced Omark's ZIPS (Zero Inventory Production System) campaign to companies across the United States. Every year, Omark presents the Shingo Award to one of its 17 facilities worldwide with the best overall improvement record for that year.

In the meantime, Productivity, Inc. acquired the American distribution rights to the English version of my book on the Toyota Production System, and vigorous promotion sent sales skyrocketing. With other orders coming directly to Japan from around the world, as of July 1985, a total of 17,000 copies have been sold.

In Sweden, the English edition of the Toyota Production System impressed Professor Lars O. Sødahl of Chalmers University, so he translated the work into Swedish and published it. Other translations have been published in France, Italy, Finland, Denmark, and Yugoslavia.

Other English translations of my books have been published by Productivity Press, including *A Revolution in Manufacturing: The SMED System*, and *Zero Quality Control: Source Inspection and the Poka-yoke System*. A newly edited version of *Study of Toyota Production System from an Industrial Engineering Standpoint* is scheduled to appear in late 1987.

Thus, my activities on behalf of production improvement have become international in scope, and three or four times a year I travel to the United States, Canada, Europe, Scandinavia, and Australia to consult, lecture, and conduct workshops.

* * * * * * *

Looking back on the path I have traveled, I see that I have learned much from my elders, through contact with friends, and from experiences actually conducting improvement surveys in production plants. I feel strongly that the new techniques I have developed have sprung from these sources and from my reflections on the lessons

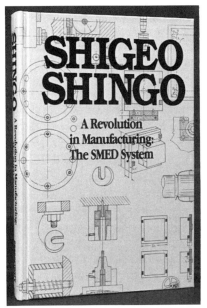
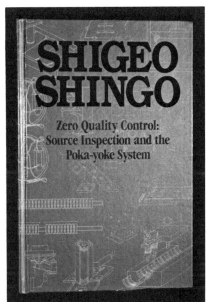

they have taught me. For this reason, I would like, once again, to express sincere thanks to those many people who have given me suggestions and critical opportunities.

In our short conversations on improvement each month, Akira Shibata, executive director of Daihō Industries, used to tell me that *know-how* alone isn't enough — you've got to have *know-why* as well. This was the first of much advice I received from Mr. Shibata. I was on a business trip in New York when I received word of his sudden passing on May 3, 1985, at the early age of 53. I was deeply grieved to see my good friend die so young.

I appreciate suggestions and insights I have received from numerous people with whom I have had daily contact; from Dr. Kōjirō Yamaoka of Shinki Kōkyū Kōki, a man of broad international perspective, and from the profoundly learned Hidebito Okajima of Toyota Auto Body. I am deeply grateful also to the many people who have provided opportunities for me to make steady progress over the years.

Finally, I would like to express my profound appreciation to Tomoyoshi Morita, my former editor, and to Ichirō Madori, my current editor, who have both been so patient working with the long series of journal articles from *Kōgyō Kanri* (Industrial Management) on which this book is based.

A FINAL NOTE

My involvement with plant improvement extends over 50 years — an involvement that began with my attendance at the Japan Industry Association's first Production Technology Seminar in 1937.

It was in that year, too, that my wife and I began a new life together.

As a professional improvement consultant for the past 20 years, I have engaged in plant surveys that have continuously kept me away from home on business for most of each year. For the behind-the-scenes support she has given my work for so long, I would like to dedicate this book to my wife.

Publications

Mr. Shingo's books have sold more than **40,000** copies worldwide. For convenience, all titles are given in English, although most have not yet been translated into English.

The improvement examples presented in *Shingo Sayings* were drawn from Mr. Shingo's broad experience as a consultant. Many appear in three of his earlier works (in Japanese):

Technology for Plant Improvement. Japan Management Association, 1955.

Views and Thoughts on Plant Improvement and *Plant Improvement Embodiments and Examples*, a two-volume set published by Nikkan Kōgyō Shimbun, Ltd., 1957.

A Systematic Philosophy of Plant Improvement. Nikkan Kōgyō Shimbun, Ltd., 1980.

Mr. Shingo's other works include:

"Ten Strategies for Smashing Counterarguments," *Sakken to Kyoryoku* [*Practice and Cooperation*], 1938.

A General Introduction to Industrial Engineering. Japan Management Association, 1949.

Improving Production Control. Nihon Keizai Shimbun, 1950.

Production Control Handbook (Process Control). Kawade Shobō, 1953.

Don't Discard New Ideas. Hakuto Shobō, 1959.

Key Issues in Process Control Improvement. Nikkan Kōgyō Shimbun, Ltd., 1962.

Issues in Plant Improvement. Nikkan Kōgyō Shimbun, Ltd., 1964.

Techniques of Machine Layout Improvement. Nikkan Kōgyō Shimbun Ltd., 1965.

Fundamental Approaches to Plant Improvement. Nikkan Kōgyō Shimbun, Ltd., 1976.

"The Toyota Production System — An Industrial Engineering Study," published serially in *Factory Management* Nikkan Kōgyō Shimbun, Ltd., 1979.

The Toyota Production System — An Industrial Engineering Study. Nikkan Kōgyō Shimbun, Ltd., 1980. (Also in English, French and Swedish, with a revised English edition forthcoming from Productivity Press.)

A Revolution in Manufacturing: The SMED System. Japan Management Association, 1983 (English edition Productivity Press, 1985).

Zero Quality Control: Source Inspection and the Poka-yoke System. Japan Management Association, 1985 (English edition Productivity Press, 1986).

"180 Proposals for Plant Improvement (Sayings of Shigeo Shingo)," published serially in *Factory Management,* Nikkan Kōgyō Shimbun, Ltd., 1980-83.

Understanding Basic Production Resources: The Essence of the Toyota Production Formula and the Challenge of Non-stock Production. Japan Management Association, in press (English edition Productivity Press, forthcoming).

Index

Books from Productivity Press

Productivity Press publishes books that empower individuals and companies to achieve excellence in quality, productivity, and the creative involvement of all employees. Through steadfast efforts to support the vision and strategy of continuous improvement, Productivity Press delivers today's leading-edge tools and techniques gathered directly from industry leaders around the world. Call toll-free (800) 394-6868 for our free catalog.

5 Pillars of the Visual Workplace
The Sourcebook for 5S Implementation
Hiroyuki Hirano

In this important sourcebook, JIT expert Hiroyuki Hirano provides the most vital information available on the visual workplace. He describes the 5S's: in Japanese they are seiri, seiton, seiso, seiketsu, and shitsuke (which translate as sort, set in order, shine, standardize, and sustain). Hirano discusses how the 5S theory fosters efficiency, maintenance, and continuous improvement in all areas of the company, from the plant floor to the sales office. This book includes case material, graphic illustrations, and photographs.
ISBN 1-56327-047-1 / 377 pages, illustrated / $85.00 / Order FIVE-B181

20 Keys to Workplace Improvement (Revised Edition)
Iwao Kobayashi

The 20 Keys system does more than just bring together twenty of the world's top manufacturing improvement approaches—it integrates these individual methods into a closely interrelated system for revolutionizing every aspect of your manufacturing organization. This revised edition of Kobayashi's bestseller amplifies the synergistic power of raising the levels of all these critical areas simultaneously. The new edition presents upgraded criteria for the five-level scoring system in most of the 20 Keys, supporting your progress toward becoming not only best in your industry but best in the world.
ISBN 1-56327-109-5 / 302 pages / $50.00 / Order 20KREV-B181

Tool Navigator
The Master Guide for Teams
Walter J. Michalski

Are you constantly searching for just the right tool to help your team efforts? Do you find yourself not sure which to use next? Here's the largest tool compendium of facilitation and problem solving tools you'll find. Each tool is presented in a two to three page spread which describes the tool, its use, how to implement it, and an example. Charts provide a matrix to help you choose the right tool for your needs. Plus, you can combine tools to help your team navigate through any problem solving or improvement process. Use these tools for all seasons: team building, idea generating, data collecting, analyzing/trending, evaluating/selecting, decision making, planning/presenting, and more!
ISBN 1-56327-178-8 / 550 pages / $150.00 / Order NAVI1-B181

Productivity Press, Dept. BK, P.O. Box 13390, Portland, OR 97213-0390
Telephone: 1-800-394-6868   Fax: 1-800-394-6286

Becoming Lean
Inside Stories of U.S. Manufacturers
Jeffrey Liker

Most other books on lean management focus on technical methods and offer a picture of what a lean system should look like. Some provide snapshots of before and after. This is the first book to provide technical descriptions of successful solutions and performance improvements. The first book to include powerful first-hand accounts of the complete process of change, its impact on the entire organization, and the rewards and benefits of becoming lean. At the heart of this book you will find the stories of American manufacturers who have successfully implemented lean methods. Authors offer personalized accounts of their organization's lean transformation, including struggles and successes, frustrations and surprises. Now you have a unique opportunity to go inside their implementation process to see what worked, what didn't, and why. Many of these executives and managers who led the charge to becoming lean in their organizations tell their stories here for the first time!
ISBN 1-56327-173-7 / 350 pages / $35.00 / Order LEAN-B181

CEDAC
A Tool for Continuous Systematic Improvement
Ryuji Fukuda

CEDAC, encompasses three tools for continuous systematic improvement: window analysis (for identifying problems), the CEDAC diagram (a modification of the classic "fishbone diagram," for analyzing problems and developing standards), and window development (for ensuring adherence to standards). This manual provides directions for setting up and using CEDAC. Sample forms included.
ISBN 1-56327-140-0 / 144 pages / $30.00 / Order CEDAC-B181

Corporate Diagnosis
Setting the Global Standard for Excellence
Thomas L. Jackson with Constance E. Dyer

All too often, strategic planning neglects an essential first step- and final step-diagnosis of the organization's current state. What's required is a systematic review of the critical factors in organizational learning and growth, factors that require monitoring, measurement, and management to ensure that your company competes successfully. This executive workbook provides a step-by-step method for diagnosing an organization's strategic health and measuring its overall competitiveness against world class standards. With checklists, charts, and detailed explanations, *Corporate Diagnosis* is a practical instruction manual. The pillars of Jackson's diagnostic system are strategy, structure, and capability. Detailed diagnostic questions in each area are provided as guidelines for developing your own self-assessment survey.
ISBN 1-56327-086-2 / 100 pages / $65.00 / Order CDIAG-B181

Productivity Press, Dept. BK, P.O. Box 13390, Portland, OR 97213-0390
Telephone: 1-800-394-6868   Fax: 1-800-394-6286

Cycle Time Management
The Fast Track to Time-Based Productivity Improvement
Patrick Northey and Nigel Southway

As much as 90 percent of the operational activities in a traditional plant are nonessential or pure waste. This book presents a proven methodology for eliminating this waste within 24 to 30 months by measuring productivity in terms of time instead of revenue or people. CTM is a cohesive management strategy that integrates just-in-time (JIT) production, computer integrated manufacturing (CIM), and total quality control (TQC). From this succinct, highly focused book, you'll learn what CTM is, how to implement it, and how to manage it.
ISBN 1-56327-015-3 / 200 pages / $30.00 / Order CYCLE-B181

Implementing a Lean Management System
Thomas L. Jackson with Karen R. Jones

Does your company think and act ahead of technological change, ahead of the customer, and ahead of the competition? Thinking strategically requires a company to face these questions with a clear future image of itself. *Implementing a Lean Management System* lays out a comprehensive management system for aligning the firm's vision of the future with market realities. Based on hoshin management, the Japanese strategic planning method used by top managers for driving TQM throughout an organization, Lean Management is about deploying vision, strategy, and policy to all levels of daily activity. It is an eminently practical methodology emerging out of the implementation of continuous improvement methods and employee involvement. The key tools of this book builds on the knowledge of the worker, multiskilling, and an understanding of the role and responsibilities of the new lean manufacturer.
ISBN 1-56327-085-4 / 182 pages / $65.00 / Order ILMS-B181

Integrating Kanban with MRPII
Automating a Pull System for Enhanced JIT Inventory Management
Raymond S. Louis

Manufacturing organizations continuously strive to match the supply of products to market demand. Now for the first time, the automated kanban system is introduced utilizing MRPII. This book describes an automated kanban system that integrates MRPII, kanban bar codes and a simple version of electronic data interchange into a breakthrough system that substantially lowers inventory and significantly eliminates non-value adding activities. This new system automatically recalculates and triggers replenishment, integrates suppliers into the manufacturing loop, and uses bar codes to enhance speed and accuracy of the receipt process. From this book, you will learn how to enhance the flexibility of your manufacturing organization and dramatically improve your competitive position.
ISBN 1-56327-182-6 / 200 pages / $45.00 / Order INTKAN-B181

Productivity Press, Dept. BK, P.O. Box 13390, Portland, OR 97213-0390
Telephone: 1-800-394-6868   Fax: 1-800-394-6286

JIT Implementation Manual
The Complete Guide to Just-In-Time Manufacturing
Hiroyuki Hirano

Encyclopedic in scope and written by a top international consultant, this comprehensive manual provides the JIT professional with the answer to virtually any JIT problem. It shows multiple options for handling every stage of implementation, is appropriate to all factory settings, and covers JIT concepts, techniques, and tools, and includes hundreds of illustrations and JIT management forms.
ISBN 0-915299-66-6 / 1500 pages / $975.00 / Order HIR1-B181

Kaizen for Quick Changeover
Going Beyond SMED
Kenichi Sekine and Keisuke Arai

Especially useful for manufacturing managers and engineers, this book describes exactly how to achieve faster changeover. Picking up where Shingo's SMED book left off, you'll learn how to streamline the process even further to reduce changeover time and optimize staffing at the same time.
ISBN 0-915299-38-0 / 315 pages / $75.00 / Order KAIZEN-B181

Manufacturing Strategy
How to Formulate and Implement a Winning Plan
John Miltenburg

This book offers a step-by-step method for creating a strategic manufacturing plan. The key tool is a multidimensional worksheet that links the competitive analysis to manufacturing outputs, the seven basic production systems, the levels of capability and the levers for moving to a higher level. The author presents each element of the worksheet and shows you how to link them to create an integrated strategy and implementation plan. By identifying the appropriate production system for your business, you can determine what output you can expect from manufacturing, how to improve outputs, and how to change to more optimal production systems as your business needs changes. This is a valuable book for general managers, operations managers, engineering managers, marketing managers, comptrollers, consultants, and corporate staff in any manufacturing company
ISBN 1-56327-071-4 / 391 pages / $45.00 / Order MANST-B181

Modern Approaches to Manufacturing Improvement
The Shingo System
Alan Robinson (ed.)

Here's the quickest and most inexpensive way to learn about the pioneering work of Shigeo Shingo, co-creator (with Taiichi Ohno) of Just-In-Time. It's an introductory book containing excerpts of five of his classic books as well as an excellent introduction by Professor Robinson. Learn about quick changeover, mistake-proofing (poka-yoke), non-stock production, and how to apply Shingo's "scientific thinking mechanism."
ISBN 0-915299-64-X / 420 pages / $23.00 paper / Order READER-B181

Productivity Press, Dept. BK, P.O. Box 13390, Portland, OR 97213-0390
Telephone: 1-800-394-6868   Fax: 1-800-394-6286

Non-Stock Production
The Shingo System for Continuous Improvement
Shigeo Shingo

In the ideal production system, information flows from the customer backward through the manufacturing process and results in total elimination of non-value-adding wastes. That means no inventory, inspection, storage, or transportation. Shingo shows that a Non-Stock Production (NSP) system can become a reality for any manufacturer. Find out how, directly from the master himself.
ISBN 0-915299-30-5 / 479 pages / $85.00 / Order NON-B181

One-Piece Flow
Cell Design for Transforming the Production Process
Kenichi Sekine

By reconfiguring your traditional assembly lines into production cells based on one-piece flow, you can drastically reduce your lead time, staffing requirements, and number of defects. Sekine examines the basic principles of process flow building, then offers detailed case studies of how various industries designed unique one-piece flow systems to meet their particular needs.
ISBN 0-915299-33-X / 308 pages / $75.00 / Order 1PIECE-B181

Poka-Yoke
Improving Product Quality by Preventing Defects
Nikkan Kogyo Shimbun Ltd. and Factory Magazine (ed.)

If your goal is 100 percent zero defects, here is the book for you—a completely illustrated guide to poka-yoke (mistake-proofing) for supervisors and shopfloor workers. Many poka-yoke devices come from line workers and are implemented with the help of engineering staff. The result is better product quality—and greater participation by workers in efforts to improve your processes, your products, and your company as a whole.
ISBN 0-915299-31-3 / 295 pages / $65.00 / Order IPOKA-B181

A Revolution in Manufacturing
The SMED System
Shigeo Shingo

The heart of JIT is quick changeover methods. Dr. Shingo, inventor of the Single-Minute Exchange of Die (SMED) system for Toyota, shows you how to reduce your changeovers by an average of 98 percent! By applying Shingo's techniques, you'll see rapid improvements (lead time reduced from weeks to days, lower inventory and warehousing costs) that will improve quality, productivity, and profits.
ISBN 0-915299-03-8 / 383 pages / $80.00 / Order SMED-B181

Productivity Press, Dept. BK, P.O. Box 13390, Portland, OR 97213-0390
Telephone: 1-800-394-6868   Fax: 1-800-394-6286

Visual Feedback Photography
Making Your 5S Implementation Click
Adapted from materials by Ken ichi Ono

Are you looking for a way to breath some life into your 5S activities in a way that vividly demonstrates your progress? Consider capturing the evolution of your program in photographs. Visual Feedback Photography is a simple method for teams to use as they implement workplace improvements, and a means to record changes in the workplace over time. The result is a series of photographs displayed on a workplace chart, providing a clear record of improvement activities related to workplace problem areas.
ISBN 1-56327-090-1 /$150.00 / Order VFPACT-B181

Zero Quality Control
Source Inspection and the Poka-Yoke System
Shigeo Shingo

Dr. Shingo reveals his unique defect prevention system, which combines source inspection and poka-yoke (mistake-proofing) devices that provide instant feedback on errors before they can become defects. The result: 100 percent inspection that eliminates the need for SQC and produces defect-free products without fail. Includes 112 examples, most costing under $100. Two-part video program also available; call for details.
ISBN 0-915299-07-0 / 328 pages / $75.00 / Order ZQC-B181

TO ORDER: Write, phone, or fax Productivity Press, Dept. BK, P.O. Box 13390, Portland, OR 97213-0390, phone 1-800-394-6868, fax 1-800-394-6286. Outside the U.S. phone (503) 235-0600; fax (503) 235-0909. Send check or charge to your credit card (American Express, Visa, MasterCard accepted).

U.S. ORDERS: Add $5 shipping for first book, $2 each additional for UPS surface delivery. Add $5 for each AV program containing 1 or 2 tapes; add $12 for each AV program containing 3 or more tapes. We offer attractive quantity discounts for bulk purchases of individual titles; call for more information.

ORDER BY E-MAIL: Order 24 hours a day from anywhere in the world. Use either address:
To order: service@ppress.com
To view the online catalog and/or order: http://www.ppress.com/

QUANTITY DISCOUNTS: For information on quantity discounts, please contact our sales department.

INTERNATIONAL ORDERS: Write, phone, or fax for quote and indicate shipping method desired. For international callers, telephone number is 503-235-0600 and fax number is 503-235-0909. Prepayment in U.S. dollars must accompany your order (checks must be drawn on U.S. banks). When quote is returned with payment, your order will be shipped promptly by the method requested.

NOTE: Prices are in U.S. dollars and are subject to change without notice.

About the Shopfloor Series

Put powerful and proven improvement tools in the hands of your entire workforce!

Progressive shopfloor improvement techniques are imperative for manufacturers who want to stay competitive and to achieve world class excellence. And it's the comprehensive education of all shopfloor workers that ensures full participation and success when implementing new programs. The Shopfloor Series books make practical information accessible to everyone by presenting major concepts and tools in simple, clear language and at a reading level that has been adjusted for operators by skilled instructional designers. One main idea is presented every two to four pages so that the book can be picked up and put down easily. Each chapter begins with an overview and ends with a summary section. Helpful illustrations are used throughout.

Books currently in the Shopfloor Series include:

5S FOR OPERATORS
5 Pillars of the Visual Workplace
The Productivity Press Development Team
ISBN 1-56327-123-0 / incl. application questions
133 pages
Order 5SOP-B181 / $25.00

QUICK CHANGEOVER FOR OPERATORS
The SMED System
The Productivity Press Development Team
ISBN 1-56327-125-7 / incl. application questions
93 pages
Order QCOOP-B181 / $25.00

MISTAKE-PROOFING FOR OPERATORS
The Productivity Press Development Team
ISBN 1-56327-127-3 / 93 pages
Order ZQCOP-B181/ $25.00

TPM FOR SUPERVISORS
The Productivity Press Development Team
ISBN 1-56327-161-3 / 96 pages
Order TPMSUP-B181 / $25.00

TPM FOR EVERY OPERATOR
Japan Institute of Plant Maintenance
ISBN 1-56327-080-3 / 136 pages
Order TPMEO-B181 / $25.00

AUTONOMOUS MAINTENANCE
Japan Institute of Plant Maintenance
ISBN 1-56327-082-X / 138 pages
Order AUTMOP-B181 / $25.00

JUST-IN-TIME FOR OPERATORS
The Productivity Press Development Team
ISBN 1-56327-133-8 / 84 pages
Order JITOP-B181 / $25.00

TPM TEAM GUIDE
Kunio Shirose
ISBN 1-56327-079-X / 175 pages
Order TGUIDE-B181/ $25.00

FOCUSED EQUIPMENT IMPROVEMENT FOR TPM TEAMS
Japan Institute of Plant Maintenance
ISBN 1-56327-081-1 / 138 pages
Order FEIOP-B181/ $25.00

Productivity Press, Dept. BK, P.O. Box 13390, Portland, OR 97213-0390
Telephone: 1-800-394-6868   Fax: 1-800-394-6286

Continue Your Learning with In-House Training and Consulting from the Productivity Consulting Group

The Productivity Consulting Group (PCG) offers a diverse menu of consulting services and training products based on the exciting ideas contained in the books of Productivity Press. Whether you need assistance with long term planning or focused, results-driven training, PCG's experienced professional staff can enhance your pursuit of competitive advantage.

PCG integrates a cutting edge management system with today's leading process improvement tools for rapid, measurable, lasting results. In concert with your management team, PCG will focus on implementing the principles of Value Adding Management, Total Quality Management, Just-In-Time, and Total Productive Maintenance. Each approach is supported by Productivity's wide array of team-based tools: Standardization, One-Piece Flow, Hoshin Planning, Quick Changeover, Mistake-Proofing, Kanban, Problem Solving with CEDAC, Visual Workplace, Visual Office, Autonomous Maintenance, Equipment Effectiveness, Design of Experiments, Quality Function Deployment, Ergonomics, and more. And, based on the continuing research of Productivity Press, PCG expands its offering every year.

Productivity is known for significant improvement on the shopfloor and the bottom line. Through years of repeat business, an expanding and loyal client base continues to recommend Productivity to their colleagues. Contact PCG to learn how we can tailor our services to fit your needs.

Telephone: 1-800-966-5423 (U.S. only) or 1-203-846-3777
Fax: 1-203-846-6883